Mind, Time & Power!

Using the hidden power
of your mind to:

- Heal your Past,
- Transform your Present,
- Create your Future

Anthony Hamilton

Mind, Time and Power! - Using the hidden power of your mind to heal your past, transform your present, create your future

ISBN 0-9686885-1-9

Third Edition
Printed in Canada

LifeWorks! Publishing
425-1020 Pembroke St.
Victoria, BC
V8T 4Z6

Mind, Time & Power!

Using the hidden power
of your mind to:

- Heal your Past,
- Transform your Present,
- Create your Future

Anthony Hamilton

Dedication

This book is dedicated to my children Alecia, Graham and Ian. You have taught me that the world is indeed a mysterious place, and a very benevolent one.

To the most influential men in my life: my father Robert, who taught me the way the world works; the Vikings, who offer me continual support, understanding and good-natured ridicule.

To the most influential women in my life: my mother, Eileen, who taught me that anything worth having is worth fighting for; Natashaw and Pauline who gave me the greatest gifts any person can give another; and most of all, Zhang Jing who taught me that I am loveable just as I am.

I owe it all to you.

PROLOGUE

I have always believed each of us was born with the power to realize our dreams. As a child, whenever I read about someone who achieved something important, I would think to myself, 'I could do that too, if I really tried.' However, over time, I found that when I really did try to achieve my goals, as often as not my efforts resulted in disappointment and frustration.

When I finally took a long, hard look at myself a number of years ago now, I had to admit that many areas of my life were more like a nightmare than a dream.

My relationships were confusing and painful. My work provided little satisfaction. I felt overworked, underpaid and unappreciated. It seemed wherever I looked, my world was filled with situations and circumstances I didn't want.

'If it's really true that each of us was born with so much power' I wondered, 'how did my life come to contain so much of what I don't want?'

My search for an answer to this question lasted more than a decade. Eventually I realized that the unwanted conditions of my life were the result of a series of unconscious choices I had been making.

In other words, I had been creating the unwanted conditions of my life -- but I had been doing so unconsciously.

To change things around required that I first of all become aware of what these choices were -- then consciously make some new ones.

In making the shift from unconsciously choosing what I don't want to consciously choosing what I do want, I discovered that I actually did have the power to determine the contents of my life, but had never been taught how to use this power.

The purpose of this book is to describe the process I went through in making this discovery and to assist you in discovering your own inner power, should you choose to do so.

Introduction

As a young man I was fascinated by people of power.

I loved reading tales of King Arthur and the Knights of the Round Table. I was especially intrigued by the magical power of Merlin the Magician.

He had extraordinary insight and wisdom and possessed the power to do things that were impossible for the average person. He could heal the sick, predict the future, make things appear or disappear, understand the inner workings of the world and unravel the secrets of the universe. This kind of 'secret' power was very appealing to me.

In the middle ages, European alchemists searched for the secret for transforming lead into gold. I too was captivated by the idea of being able to transform an ordinary substance into something of great value and power.

In high school I realized that the founders of modern science - Copernicus, Kepler, Gallileo, Newton - began their careers as alchemists and became scientists as they learned to explain their discoveries with newly formulated laws of physics and chemistry

instead of magic formulas and superstitions.

Their work created science from the fires of the alchemists' cauldrons. These early alchemist-scientists bridged the gap between the magicians of old and the giants of the modern scientific age - Rutherford, Edison, Marconi and Bell.

The most famous of these early scientists was Isaac Newton, a brilliant 17th century thinker who formulated laws of gravity and motion. These modern scientists have something in common with the ancient magicians and alchemists - the ability to see the connection between the world of the mind and the world of matter.

They have discovered that the *transformation of the world* is always preceded by the transformation of an *idea*.

The most famous of these modern scientists, Albert Einstein, transformed Newton's ideas of time and space, coining the phrase *space-time continuum* to explain that the laws of space and the laws of time are mirror images of each other.

Since one characteristic of the human mind is its connection to both the past and the future, I wondered if Einstein's ideas of time might also be applied to the mind, meaning that a psychology based on the work of Newton could be replaced by a psychology based on the work of Einstein.

If so, this would bring into play the power of the future as a creative force. This seemingly bizarre idea made intuitive sense to me. 'After all' I thought, 'isn't it true that to succeed in life we must know which possible future we want to experience?' In short, we need a *dream to create*.

Whether our creativity is manifested in the arts, in business, politics, sports or science, are not those of us with power those who know what dreams we want to make real?

Does not our dream create a *connection* to our chosen future and provide the information, the inspiration and the motivation that keeps us going when people lacking a dream run out of steam?

I realized that the *power of a goal* is that it tells us how it can be achieved -- if we will but ask the right questions.

And of course, a goal is in the future. So here was a clear example to me of how the *future* could be used as a *source of information and power*.

In the course of my own personal journey I have come to realize that we are all alchemists.

We all have the power to transform ordinary experiences into extraordinary lessons. We can transform our failures into sources of power. We can transform ourselves from ordinary people into people of extraordinary patience, love, wisdom and compassion.

A 21st Century Psychology

I believe the transformation from a 17th century psychology to a 21st century psychology is an idea whose time has come.

I believe it is time for each of us to realize that we were born to be co-creators, to participate in a great river of unfolding manifestation which began before we drew our first breath and which will continue long after we are gone.

If we are to claim the power we were born with, we each need to begin by *transforming our vision of ourselves*. We need to see ourselves as people of power.

I came to realize that the life I wanted to create was *calling to me*, trying to manifest itself through me, if only I had the courage to accept responsibility for living my dream.

I believe the same is true for you.

If you have a vision of a life you would like to create, I believe the power to create your dream is lying within you right now, waiting to be claimed, if you will have the courage to accept it.

Can you do that? Can you accept that you have within you the power to create your dream?

If you can, I promise you an exciting and eventful journey. The path to the future of your choice will be at times confusing, at times frustrating, at times frightening. But it will never be boring. If you will persist in the belief that you deserve to be happy, that you deserve to be fulfilled, that you deserve love, I believe that one day you will wake up as I did to realize that the life you have dreamed about is happening to you now.

Anthony Hamilton
Victoria, British Columbia
November, 2009.

TABLE OF CONTENTS

Part One - Discovering Your Hidden Power

Part Two - Using Your Hidden Power

Chapter One

The Magician Within

I can sing a rainbow.

Graham Hamilton

 You were born with the power to create the life you want.

But if you are like most people, your life at the moment contains a number of situations and circumstances you don't want….and at the same time, lots of things you do want are not yet a part of your life, even though you may have tried long and hard to achieve them.

This leads to an obvious question… "If I have so much creative power, why does my life contain so many things I don't want and why have I failed to achieve the goals I do want?"

The answer to this question is deceptively simple: Your life is the way it is because up to now, your creative power has been working UNCONSCIOUSLY. In order to change things you will need to become aware of this power and learn to re-direct it CONSCIOUSLY. As you do this, you will stop creating things you don't want and begin experiencing more of what you do want.

In doing this you will become aware of a power you were born with but which you have never learned to use.

The purpose of this book is to describe what I discovered in making the shift from unconsciously creating what I don't want to consciously creating what I do want and to help you in making a similar change, if you care to do so.

The key to the whole process is to realize that the secret power we are talking about lies in the CREATIVE POWER OF YOUR THOUGHTS.

1

Put simply, YOUR THOUGHTS CREATE YOUR LIFE. Because most of your thoughts are unconscious, you are doing a lot of unconscious creating. Your job from now on will be to become more conscious of your thinking and learn how to plant into your mind specific kinds of thoughts, so that the process turns around.

This is easier said than done, as you will find out.

Developing your personal power

Down through the ages many masters have spoken of developing this kind of power and their advice has always been the same - *know thyself.*

They meant that the key to mastery over the <u>outer world</u> is gaining mastery over the <u>inner self</u> - to choose for ourselves <u>what we think</u> and <u>how we feel</u>.

The rewards of developing this power are personal happiness, peace of mind and worldly success. But developing this degree of mastery takes discipline. The journey to the inner self is not for the faint of heart.

This book outlines a system to develop the power to transform various aspects of your life, so you will be able to remove what makes you unhappy and put in what makes you happy.

As you study the concepts, do the exercises and practice the techniques, you will find that your awareness, your control and your power grow. You will discover that you really do have the ability to create conditions and circumstances of your choosing. The key to the entire process lies in learning to use your mind in a way that may be quite different from what you have been taught before.

We each live in two worlds

The first step is to realize that the mind operates simultaneously in <u>two worlds</u> - an outer, physical world of events and an inner, world of thoughts. Like a cat perched on a windowsill, your conscious awareness sits at the interface of both worlds, looking both outward and inward.

2

Sometimes your awareness is directed outward, to the physical world, making you conscious of what's going on around you. At other times it's directed inward, to the world of thought, making you conscious of what you are thinking. Most of the time you are not really conscious of either. This causes problems.

Because we have blind spots in both worlds, the relationship between these two worlds is not easy to figure out. There are aspects of both worlds we are simply not aware of.

At first glance the outer world seems separate from the inner world. But this is an illusion. The two are intimately connected. In fact, your two worlds are really just different aspects of one overall reality reflecting something going on very deep inside of you. Your job from now on will be to figure out what that "something" is.

Perception and reality

What we call our "reality" comes down to what and how we perceive it. What we perceive in the outer world is a reflection of what we conceive in the inner world. Our beliefs about reality influence our experience and perception of reality. Our perception of reality is distorted and influenced by what we think and how we think.

One clue to this whole idea of "connection" is to explore the nature of our private, innermost FEELINGS.

Most people's feelings are simply a reaction to what happens in their outer world. At first, this seems obvious - something happens to us and we feel either good or bad about it, so we naturally think our feelings are caused by what has happened.

But this is another illusion.

Our feelings are not caused by what happens but by the meaning we attach to what happens. Since ultimately the meaning of any event is chosen by each of us, (usually unconsciously) our feelings are really the result of our thinking...not of the event itself.

3

We may perceive and even believe that events cause our feelings, but the reality is quite different. As you learn to give each event a positive meaning (and a positive feeling) your world will undergo a profound shift. Cultivating the skill of consciously giving events a positive meaning will be one of your main tasks from now on.

How your two worlds affect each other

 That the outer world can affect the inner world seems obvious. What might not be so obvious is that THE CONNECTION GOES BOTH WAYS. In other words, our thinking affects the outer world!

The process that brings this about is quite subtle, but we can easily prove it to ourselves because any time we change an attitude the world shifts. The fact that you can change your reaction (and your feeling) about any outer event will give you proof your thinking can affect your world. Doing this with control can take considerable insight and awareness.

The good news is that to create our desires as physical realities we don't need to change the world. We need only change our thinking. The outer world will then be transformed automatically. Changing your thinking changes both your worlds!

Two sets of awareness - two sets of senses

As we examine the outer world our OUTER AWARENESS gathers information using our OUTER SENSES. As we examine the inner world, our INNER AWARENESS gathers information using our INNER SENSES.

The operation of the inner awareness is subtle. When it gathers information from the past we call it <u>memory</u>. When it gathers information from the future we may call it <u>day-dreaming</u> (if the information is positive) or <u>worrying</u> (if the information is negative). But the inner awareness is always operating, gathering information

4

form different areas of our inner world, and most of the time we are not conscious of what it is doing or how it is doing it.

To consciously direct the inner awareness so it gathers specific information from specific areas of the past or the future is a major aspect of the your new skill of <u>conscious co-creation</u> and can take considerable effort to master.

A later chapter gives a detailed description of the INNER FIELD OF TIME in which the inner awareness moves. You will receive specific instructions on how to move your awareness around within this inner field of time. How well you develop this skill determines whether you become a victim of circumstances or a creator of them.

Controlling the movements of your inner awareness is THE MASTER KEY which unlocks a storehouse of inner knowledge and power. As we bring various aspects of the past and future into the present to be examined, we discover that we have everything we need to heal the past and create our dreams.

Matter and energy are two sides of the same coin

Einstein's famous equation, $E=mc^2$ shows that matter, energy, time and space are simply four different aspects of one overall reality. Scientists now understand that

- the physical and the non-physical are connected,
- knowledge depends upon belief,
- the observer influences the results of every experiment,
- expectations influence the conditions we encounter.

Magicians have always known this.

Ultimately the power to transform your reality depends upon your belief. Your power is only as strong as you believe it is. How much creative power do you believe you have today? Are you prepared to do the necessary work to change this belief?

We each have two brains

In the mid 1970's a scientist in California named Roger Sperry performed a remarkable experiment. In an effort to cure a patient's epilepsy, he cut a bundle of nerves connecting the two halves of the patient's brain. As a result, Sperry came to realize that we don't actually have one brain. We have two! He also discovered these two brains do quite different things.

After the patient's brains were cut, Sperry discovered that the patient could talk about what he held in his <u>right</u> hand because this hand was still connected to the language center in the <u>left</u> brain. But he couldn't talk about what he held in his left hand because the operation had severed the connection to the language centre.

Sperry discovered that using his <u>left</u> hand, the patient could draw a picture of an object previously held in this hand. This proved that his right brain retained the memory. But because his brains were now divided, different information was held by each brain! His right hand literally didn't know what his left hand was doing! When asked, "Do you know what you are holding in your left hand?" his head nodded <u>Yes</u> while his mouth said, <u>No</u>!

The source of your inner conflict

Sperry's discovery gives us insight into the conflict we each experience when we <u>feel</u> something to be true that our thinking says is false or when we <u>feel</u> we want something but <u>think</u> we don't deserve it.

The conflict between thinking and feeling creates endless problems for each of us. It interferes with our ability to achieve happiness and success. It makes us chase after things we think will make us happy and blinds us to the treasures we already possess. It tricks us into behaviors we know are unhealthy as though we are driven by some unseen force. As our private, inner conflict spills over to affect our public, outer world, it makes our lives a confusing jumble of conflicting beliefs, behaviors, emotions, desires and fears.

6

To erase our conflicts and create harmony in our world we need to control both our thinking and our feelings. This can be tricky.

Regaining the balance in our lives

To regain balance in our lives and access our personal power, we each need to embark upon a private, inner journey, following a private inner logical and emotional path. We need to investigate, understand and exercise both our brains.

During the course of this journey, we'll come to discover what we really want, how we really think and what we truly believe. We'll discover what we feel and why we feel it. As we progress on the path we'll recapture the sense of wonder we experienced as a child, when fantasy and reality were one. We'll also discover a great wellspring of creative power lying within us waiting to be tapped. Harmony within will create harmony without.

For each of us, the journey both begins and ends with gaining an increased knowledge of ourselves. We begin by sorting out our thinking and sorting out the various pieces of our lives. Then we need to put them back together again so they fit together in a new way. We need to take ourselves apart and put ourselves back together again.

A magical process

This is not simply a book about positive thinking. Instead, it is a guide book for your own personal voyage of self-discovery and a hand book for coming into conscious cooperation with the creative forces of the universe.

Your success in creating the external conditions you desire will depend upon your gaining an increased awareness of yourself and your power. Since your personal journey involves a re-examination of both your inner and your outer worlds, the program outlined in these   pages has a dual nature to it.

7

The first aspect of this process involves discovering the source of your creative power and learning how to use it. The second involves deciding what goals you want to create for yourself and deciding what kind of person you would like to become. This is vital. Since your external circumstances will always reflect your inner nature, the new reality you create will really be a reflection of the new person you are becoming.

What type of work do you want? What kind of lifestyle do you wish to live? What type of man or woman do you wish as a partner? How healthy do you wish to be? What effect would you like to have upon your family, upon your community, and upon your world? How can you achieve your own happiness?

As you progress through this book you will discover your own answers to these questions.

Although the information in this book is organized into chapters, it actually revolves around five main themes which weave throughout the text. You will encounter different aspects of each of them in various places throughout the book.

These five themes are:

- Motivation,
- Attitude,
- Goals,
- Imagination,
- Consciousness,

The first letters of each of these words, taken together, spell "MAGIC"

This word represents five powerful skills you must master if you are to consciously create the life you want. I'll briefly discuss each of these in turn.

Motivation

A motive is actually two things at once. Firstly, it is a <u>reason</u> to act. Secondly, it is a <u>force</u> for movement.

To persevere along our chosen path we must know both <u>what</u> we want and <u>why</u> we want it. A clear idea of WHY we want something transforms our <u>intention</u> into a <u>force</u> which propels us from one reality to another.

Attitude

Attitudes do several things at once. They <u>filter</u> thoughts, so we think more of one kind of thought and less of another. They <u>shape</u> our perceptions, so we notice different kinds of things in both the inner and outer worlds. They <u>give meaning</u>, <u>form</u> and <u>texture</u> to both our worlds. Our attitudes determine both the <u>conditions</u> we meet and the <u>emotions</u> we feel. When we expect resistance we encounter it. When we think ourselves unworthy of success we feel frustrated wanting something we think we don't deserve.

To work with your attitudes means to work with a form of energy most people are simply unaware of. To consciously choose attitudes that work for you allows you to create both <u>new opportunities</u> and <u>new emotions</u>.

Attitudes form patterns which can be discovered and changed. In a later chapter we will explore a powerful method for uncovering and altering these patterns. You will learn to delete negative attitudes and insert positive attitudes. When we adopt the attitude that success comes from doing what we enjoy, the more fun we have, the more success we experience. Changing your attitude about life changes your life.

Goals

To design our destiny means to decide the ultimate meaning of our lives - to live life on our terms. If we don't know what we want we will never have the power to create it nor will we feel satisfied with what we already have. We can use our left brains to sort out the pieces of our lives and our right brains to choose new patterns for them. We can create a written plan that serves as a road map to the future of our choice. Doing this will focus our mind, balance our personality, rid us of stress and keep us physically and emotionally healthy. As we continue this process we discover that anything we can imagine in our inner world we can experience in our outer world.

Imagination

The imagination is the connecting link between the inner and outer worlds. The ability to control your imagination is the mark of the master. People with no control over their imagination get trapped in worry. This makes them victims of their thinking. They end up experiencing inner realities that don't exist physically.

The most valuable talent each of us can develop is the ability to hold in our mind a clear image of a desired situation while holding in our body a positive feeling about it. This skill connects us to an unlimited wellspring of positive energy that helps bring the imagined situation about. Control creates power. Controlling our imagination enables us to use our thinking and our feelings as creative forces, bringing into being the realities we want to create.

Consciousness

Even though the earth exists at one point in space, its gravity reaches to the farthest edge of the universe. In a similar manner, your body exists at one point in time but your thinking reaches to the farthest limits of your past and your future.

Your conscious mind straddles the boundary between the physical and the non-physical. You have the ability to hold in your mind thoughts of the outer world, thoughts of the inner world, or both simultaneously.

As the focus of your awareness moves from the inner world to the outer and back again, your emotions become forces that either draw your desires to you or keep them away. What each of us actually creates depends upon the strength of our motivation, the pattern of our attitudes, the clarity of our goals, the mastery of our imagination and the cultivation of our consciousness.

10

Cultivating your skills in these five areas will give you the power to achieve your goals, as well as to experience happiness, health, wealth, peace of mind, harmony in your relationships and success in your world. You will gain freedom from fear and the ability to both give and receive love. People will begin to recognize you as a champion. You will become a force in the world.

As we progress on this personal journey of awakening, we discover that each of us has a magician inside of us. As we gain access to the power of this inner magician our power increases and our lives become magic.

Chapter Two

What is_ Thinking, Anyway?

> *Row, row, row your boat, gently down the stream...*
> *merrily, merrily, merrily, merrily... life is but a*
> *dream.*
>
> Child's Nursery Rhyme

Since the purpose of this book is to give you more power over the way your life is unfolding and since I've already said that the key to this power lies in gaining increased control over your thinking, I'd better define what I mean by the term, "thinking" so we are on the same page. What is thinking, and what happens in your mind when you think? Here is a definition we can use...

> *Thinking is the process of constructing*
> *a model of reality in order to understand your experience.*

The following story will illustrate what I mean.

Imagine that you and I are sitting in a coffee shop one day and I begin telling you of a picnic I had the previous Thursday with a friend of mine in a grassy field by a local river. Imagine too that I tell you this friend brought her Irish Setter along. In order to understand my story, you need to understand the terms, *last Thursday, field, river, picnic, friend, Irish Setter,* and so on... otherwise you won't know what I'm talking about.

But of course you do understand these words. And as you sit listening to me, you unconsciously construct in your mind's eye a mental model of the scene I'm describing. You see us sitting by the river having a picnic, with the dog playing near by.

This is what thinking is ... creating a model of reality in order to understand your experience. Your experience in this case is listening to me tell my story and the model you created is your little internal movie, or "mental snapshot" of our picnic.

Because this internal activity is automatic, you don't consciously think about the fact the picnic you see in your mind is not the actual one that took place, that it's only a model. You don't actually see my friend, the river, the grass, the dog, or the picnic area. You just see internal representations of them with your inner senses.

Now, suppose we meet each other on the street again the next day and I'm pushing a young, blind lady in a wheelchair, as her seeing-eye dog walks alongside. As I introduce you, you suddenly realize she's the friend I had the picnic with.

As soon as this realization hits you, you replace your original mental picture with a new one. This gives you a new understanding of my story, because you didn't originally imagine my friend to be blind, or in a wheelchair, or that her dog was a seeing-eye dog. (As a matter of fact, the same process might have just happened as you read this anecdote... did it?)

This story illustrates my point.

This process of internal model making and re-making is usually completely unconscious. Since we don't normally get the kind of feedback as you did in my example, we normally aren't aware of how inaccurate our internal mental models are. (Let's face it: if you hadn't met the two of us on the street the next day you might never have known that your original conception of our picnic was totally inaccurate.)

Because the process is automatic and unconscious, after you've constructed one of these concepts, you store it away ready to be used again later without realizing that it's inaccurate.

13

You can use the same concepts over and over again for years…never realizing that your idea of something may be quite different from the thing being referred to.

This story illustrates what happens inside each of us. We construct models of reality called concepts to try and understand our experience, while remaining completely unaware that our internal models may contain completely false information.

Many times the differences between our concepts of reality and actual reality don't matter much. But understanding the process of constructing these models is absolutely vital. The differences between your model of reality and your actual reality lies at the root of some fundamental aspects of your life. If you don't understand this process, you won't understand why your life isn't working, and you won't be able to change things for the better. You'll continue to think the problem lies in the world when it really lies in the way you think about the world.

If you don't wake up to what's going on inside of you, you may live the rest of your life trying to change the outer world instead of changing your thinking!

Your mind has lots of concepts and models in it

One goal of this book is to wake you up to the fact that these mental models exist and have a huge impact on your life.

Here are some examples of concepts already existing in your mind.

A concept called your *self-image* determines what you can and can't do.

A concept called the *world* determines what is possible and impossible.

A concept called your *past* generates feelings and emotions in you.

A concept called your *future* determines what is likely to happen to you.

A concept called *other people* influences how you interact with people.

14

A concept called your *mind* determines how it operates, what information it contains and some of the things it can and can't do.

It's important to realize three things about your inner concepts:

- that they <u>exist</u>;
- that they are <u>false</u>;
- that they can be <u>changed</u>.

Many of your mental models were created by you as a child and are highly inaccurate. To develop your power you need to realize that they are there, that they can be changed and learn how to change them. When you succeed in changing your thinking, new possibilities, new powers and new abilities become available to you.

Much of the work of developing your personal power comes down to becoming conscious of some of your unique, automatic thought patterns, then changing them until the new pattern becomes automatic in turn.

Start paying attention to your thinking. Try to notice the kinds of concepts that exist in your mind. Simply being aware of them will take you a long way on the road to increasing your personal power.

As you investigate your inner world and change things around a bit, you will discover that you have talents and abilities you never thought existed. You'll discover that the world is quite different from what you imagined, that other people operate in ways you didn't realize, and you'll discover that the key to getting what you want in life is quite different from what you thought.

Chapter Three

Wake Up to Your Power

*Nothing determines who we
will become so much as the
things we choose to ignore.*

Sandor McNab

Why your life is the way it is

Whether you are *conceiving* your inner world or *perceiving*
your outer one, you are using the <u>same nerves</u>. A continuous
feedback loop connects your inner world and your outer one as your
mind is constantly projecting your internal models outward, where
you experience them as <u>external reality</u>. This leads to the basic
illusion I spoke of in the first chapter. The contents and
characteristics of your outer world are shaped by the contents and
characteristics of your inner world.

When a couple walking in the park sees a large German
Shepherd dog running toward them, one person becomes afraid
while the other begins to smile. Each person thinks he is reacting to
the same *physical* dog. In fact, they are reacting to different *mental*
ones.

You have been largely unaware of this process until now and
have paid little attention to the contents of your mind. Yet the
circumstances of your life reflect what is going on inside of you.
The qualities and characteristics of the contents of your mind are
constantly being projected outward, appearing to you as qualities
and characteristics of the physical world.

If you believe in obstacles you will encounter them.

If you believe in angels you will see evidence for them.

If you believe people respect you, you will feel respected.

If you believe other people are against you, you will encounter resistance.

As long as you remain blind to this on-going feedback system, you'll accept the negative aspects of your life as things you simply have to put up with. But It doesn't have to be this way. When you change your mental models your life will change.

You have as much freedom to choose the contents of your life as you do to choose the furniture in your home. But if no one has shown you how to exercise this choice, you won't have this power. As you begin to control your thinking, you will gain creative power over the contents of your life.

There are many levels of unconscious thoughts and many ways to consciously influence them. The basic skill is to become aware of the patterns which already exist in your mind and to gain a measure of control over them.

Changing your personal reality

Until now you've considered your world to consist of events. You've focused your attention on trying to produce more of the events you want while avoiding those you don't. But this isn't the way it works. You've been focusing your efforts in the wrong place

Your personal reality is not so much made up of events but of your perceptions and the meaning you attach to these perceptions. When you take apart this unconscious network of perception and meaning you discover that your past, your present and your future have changed. Events haven't changed but your life has!

This is personal transformation in the true sense. Exercising this power leads to a new understanding of your past, since memories that used to trigger pain now trigger pleasure. It changes your future, since what formerly intimidated you now excites you. Over time, as your thinking changes, your external circumstances begin to line up with the new pattern of perception and meaning laid down by your new thought patterns.

As you wake up to your power to make these kinds of changes you realize that the activity of both your brains is intertwined like two snakes fighting. It's difficult to tell if your <u>thoughts</u> are leading your <u>feelings</u> or your feelings are leading your thoughts. To separate the activity of each brain requires insight and awareness. The best way to gain this insight and maintain this awareness is to begin keeping a journal in which you keep track of certain kinds of ideas. I'll explain more of how to do this as we go.

Unconscious thought patterns

Working with unconscious thought patterns involves working with powerful forces of which most people are blind. When you know what to look for you can see their effects everywhere. From now on begin to notice the following kinds of thought patterns:

Images

If I ask you the color of your favorite shirt you can tell me, proving you have a visual memory. Yet many people are blind to the flow of imagery constantly playing just beneath the surface of their awareness. Write this statement on a card and carry it with you so you'll be reminded of it on a continuous basis: *My ability to visualize is improving daily.* This will prepare you for the visualization training you will be doing shortly.

Self Talk

You have a little voice carrying on continuously just below the surface of your awareness. Sometimes this voice says things you don't want to hear. Unless you take control, these unwanted comments can affect you in ways you don't want. Learning to change the <u>content</u> and the <u>tone</u> of this internal voice is a very powerful way to influence your internal and your external world.

Denial

Have you ever noticed yourself thinking something like, *"It looks like such and such is true, but that wouldn't make sense, so I*

18

must be mistaken.'"? The decision to ignore information that doesn't fit with your beliefs is an unconscious mechanism your mind uses to avoid painful feelings. Denial is very influential in creating the unwanted conditions you have been experiencing up to now. Catching yourself doing this will become one of your most powerful tools in creating the life you want. Failing to notice yourself doing it will keep you from developing any real power.

Negative feelings

Your feelings provide a vital clue to the thinking patterns of your right brain. Learning to control them is one of the most important keys to developing your power. We think of ourselves as logical beings because much of our thinking seems to happen in a logical sequence. But feelings are different. They aren't logical. They endure over time, influencing the content of your experience. You can feel good for a few minutes, angry for days or depressed for weeks. The shock of a powerful negative event might effect you for years. On the other hand, a friendly glance from a stranger can cause your feelings to shift in an instant.

Intuitions, emotions and states

It's important to pay attention to your feelings since how you feel affects how you think. We can divide feelings into three categories: **intuitions, emotions and states**, each one more intense and exercising more control over your life.

Intuitions are subtle nudges, giving you valuable insights helping you make choices.

Emotions are powerful forces which affect your thinking and your perceptions. They influence your memory of the past and your expectations for the future. They affect your perceptions of your past, your present and your future. Things which mean one thing when you're feeling *up* can mean something entirely different when you're feeling *down*. Emotions create self-fulfilling prophesies. You'll expect less success when you're feeling down than when you're feeling confident.

19

It is a great mistake to deny your negative feelings and dismiss them as of no importance. Emotionalized thoughts are powerful creative forces. One moment of anger can destroy a relationship you have spent years nurturing.

States are intense emotions that charge your entire being for good or for ill. Some examples of states are anger, fear, confidence, being in love. Although any emotion will influence your thinking to a certain degree, an intense state can transform a heaven into a hell or a hell into a heaven.

We consider states so important that we even identify people by their states. We call one person a *worrier*, another an *optimist*, a third *scatterbrained*. These terms also describe the worlds in which these people live, since each person's life reflects their predominant states. Developing and maintaining a set of positive states not only allows you to enjoy the present. It also allows you to remember more positive things in the past and to expect more positive things in the future. A state of self-confidence increases the chances of bringing your positive expectations into your life as physical realities.

The underlying premise of this book is not simply that you *can* create your reality but that you *are* creating it right now, unconsciously! Unconscious mental images, self-talk, feelings, intuitions, emotions and states are powerful forces which are creating definite effects in your life today. Becoming aware of them gives you insight into why your life is the way it is and provides you with powerful tools to begin changing it. As you wake up to the existence of these unconscious thought forces, you wake up your power to influence both your inner and your outer worlds.

Chapter Four

Concepts, Models and Maps

*There are more things in
heaven and earth than are
dreamt of in your philosophy.*
Shakespeare

Maps of reality

All your life you have been unconsciously constructing concepts in an effort to understand your experience and have assembled these concepts into complicated interactive networks called *cognitive maps*. You believe each concept, model and map accurately represents aspects of the world. This is an illusion.

If a person likes dogs, it's because his concept *dog* has pleasant qualities associated to it. If he doesn't like dogs, it's because his concept has unpleasant qualities. In neither case do his feelings have anything to do with dogs. Instead, they are a reaction to the qualities of his internal concept. Every time you meet a dog the feelings you experience are due to the non-physical dog in your mind, not the physical one in the world. This is true for every experience you have.

When you gaze into the world, you expect it to have the characteristics of your model. If your expectations are realized, you feel comfortable. If not, you feel some degree of discomfort. This triggers your *explainer* to generate a theory (called a *belief*) to explain the differences. In this way you learn to feel comfortable in the world and develop a set of beliefs to make sense of it.

Normally, the entire process of constructing mental models, associating characteristics to them, recognizing their physical

21

counterparts in the world, comparing the two, experiencing feelings and generating beliefs is an automatic, modularized activity to which we are completely blind. These inner actions are as unconscious as those involved in triggering images and feelings in you as read. As your eyes scan the patterns formed by the ink, you simply experience the sensations.

In a similar way, each of us thinks we are perceiving, experiencing and understanding the world when we are really experiencing the actions of our mind as it projects our expectations onto the world. As we become more aware of the contents of our inner world and the action of our mind we gain insight into how changing this internal activity, leads to a different experience of the world.

Maps of space

 A network of interlocking maps of *space* help you understand relationships between aspects of your world. You have an inner map of your city, your country, the world and the solar system. And you understand the relationship between them all. These inner maps are not very accurate. Information is generalized, distorted or deleted altogether. Distances, shapes and relationships are wrong. But a map doesn't have to be accurate to be useful.

When you drive to work, the route you visualize doesn't contain the same buildings, trees or streets as the route you drive. But it helps you get to work, so it's done its job. Likewise, your cognitive map of the solar system helps you understand where Venus is, but your conception of Venus is quite different from the physical reality of the place.

Maps of time

Maps of *time* help you organize the events of your life. You have an inner representation of your childhood, your teen-age years, your twenties, and so on. These temporal maps are also very distorted and generate feelings when you think of them. Huge areas of your past contain virtually no detail at all but you never notice the blank spots. If asked, *Can you remember your childhood?* you say *yes*, because you have a concept of it. But most of the data from those years is simply not there.

If asked, *How did you like high school?* a flood of sounds, images and feelings washes over you. You think the feelings are due to the *events* that took place. This is an illusion. They are due entirely to the characteristics of your mental map.

You also have an unconscious map of your future. It represents what you think will happen and what you you'll have to do to reach your goals. Although your concept of the future is quite different from what will actually happen, the feelings it generates determine how you set about trying to accomplish things and determines how you react to the results of your efforts.

Your internal maps of your past, present and future are no more accurate than your map of the route to work. Problems arise because you forget you have them. You think your problems are due to what's happening in the world, when they are really due to what's happening in your mental model of it.

The source of all our problems

We are all trapped in the same vicious cycle. We construct models of the world to understand it, then our models distort our experience of the very thing they're supposed to help us understand. This inevitably leads to situations where life doesn't match our expectations, leading to confusion and pain. We explain these away in order to feel better, but since our explanations are also based on distorted models, they don't solve the underlying problem. The very strategies we use to avoid negative feelings create more unwanted circumstances and more negative feelings, until our image of how life works becomes so out of alignment with reality nothing seems to make any sense.

23

Because we are reacting to a *model* of the world we think is
reality, we convince ourselves that the problem lies outside of us
when the source of our difficulties is a mental process we don't even
know exists. We try to live our lives as best we can, struggling to
make reality conform to our model of it, producing more stress,
more frustration and more disappointment. We try to avoid negative
feelings by avoiding negative situations. But since our feelings are
not caused by situations but by our thinking, our efforts don't work.
Is it any wonder we sometimes feel overwhelmed?

The solution to all our problems

Most of the difficulties we experience in life stem from the fact
that the concepts, models and maps we are using to understand the
world are wrong. The way we *think* the world operates is out of
step. Our problems are not due to past events, the actions of other
people, or the way the world works. They are due entirely to our
inaccurate mental models.

To solve our problems and develop our personal power, we
need to shift the focus of our efforts. We need to stop trying to
change the world, and instead change the way we *think* about the
world. We need to concentrate on changing the concepts, models
and maps that make up our model of the world. From now on most
of our efforts will involve working with these internal structures.

As you read the following chapters, some of the tasks you'll
undertake and some of the skills you'll develop will be considered
impossible by other people because they don't fit their model of
reality. But as you set about modifying your internal reality, your
external reality will undergo a profound shift. You'll develop a new
feeling of power, discover abilities you never knew you had, and see
opportunities for happiness and success to which you have been
blind your entire life.

Chapter Five

Adopting a New Model

*I am never discouraged, because
every wrong attempt discarded is
another step forward.*

Thomas Edison

Is the world a process or thing?

A model can be defined either by its *function* or by its *properties* and the information conveyed by the model depends upon this distinction. To define something by its function conveys *limits*. To define something by its properties conveys *possibilities*.

If I define the word *hammer* by its function, I might say, *A hammer is used to drive nails into a piece of wood.* Whether you visualize a shape like a hammer or a like a potato doesn't matter much.

But say I define the hammer by its properties. I might say, It's made of metal, shaped like a 'T', about a foot long, weighs about three pounds, has a flat metal end on one side of the 'T' and two metal prongs on the other.

This definition not only conveys a different *picture* of the hammer, it implies a number of new possible *functions*. Hearing this definition might make you realize that in addition to hitting nails, a hammer could be used to pry open a can of paint. This possibility is something the image of a potato won't convey.

The limitations you have experienced in your life to this point are due entirely to the limitations of the models you are using to think about your life. Many of these limitations are due simply to the fact that you have defined many concepts as *things* when they are *processes*. Adopting a new definition not only makes these limitations disappear, it may stimulate you to find ways of doing things you may have thought impossible before.

As you begin to see things differently, your life begins to take on a new tone. You begin to display a new level of personal power, success and self-esteem. You begin to feel a new level of confidence. Observing your new successes, some people will simply say you are lucky. This will be their explainer talking, trying to make them feel better. But you'll know the truth ... that you have built yourself a different model of reality, one containing a picture of you as a person of power.

Making a sandwich ... a model as a thing

Picture a building site at lunch time. The whistle blows and two workers, Tony and Bruno, sit down to eat. Each opens his lunch box and pulls out a paper bag with sandwiches and a thermos of coffee. As Bruno unwraps his sandwiches he becomes agitated.

Good grief, he says, Bologna again! I always get bologna sandwiches. I hate bologna sandwiches! Then, resigned that he has no choice, he begins to eat.

Tony turns to him and says, If you hate bologna so much, why don't you ask your wife to make you something else for lunch?

What do you mean? says Bruno, I always make my own lunch!

 We laugh at this story because it seems ridiculous that someone would make something he doesn't like and then complain about it. We consider ourselves intelligent enough to change a behavior that doesn't produce the desired results. But as just pointed out, the difficulties we encounter in life are caused by the models and maps we ourselves have made, so the source of our frustration is created by each of us.

You experience disappointment just as Bruno does. You settle for less than you want out of life. You feel badly about certain events in your past, feel upset by certain people in your present and are afraid of certain situations in the future. You accept these things as inevitable parts of life, but this is not life! *This is your model of life!* The frustration you feel is not due to events, people or situations. It is due to your internal models.

If you believe anything in your past, present or future has the power to make you feel badly, you've made the same mistake Bruno has.

But before you feel insulted, realize you haven't had much choice. You've been using a set of concepts and models handed down to you by others and have had virtually no choice but to construct your understanding of life from the material available to you. However you'd be shortchanging yourself if once shown a better way, you continued using the same models and continued having the same negative feelings.

Any unpleasant situation that persists in your life does so *because of the model of reality you are using.* You can discard this model and replace it with a new one, as soon as you have a new one to replace it with. I'll soon give you a series of new concepts you can use to erase your negative feelings and which will also give you fresh insight into some talents and abilities you've not been aware of until now.

But before we get to that, consider this next example.

Driving to work ... a model as a process

Picture Bruno and Tony having lunch again the next day. Still eating a bologna sandwich, Bruno turns to Tony and says, *That construction on Tenth Avenue is tearing the heck out of my suspension.*

Yeah, Tony replies, I know what you mean. I've been taking Ninth Avenue all week.

Bruno turns to Tony in disbelief, What? You mean you can get to work driving along Ninth Avenue?

Of course, replies Tony. You can get here on any street that runs east and west.

Bruno's jaw drops. Gee. he says, What do you know about that?

This is another ridiculous example of an obvious point. We know driving to work is a *process* that can be accomplished a thousand different ways. Bruno's problem is that he thinks of the drive to work as a *thing*. In doing so he fails to see how easily it can be changed.

There are several noteworthy differences between things and processes. Things have parts; processes don't. Things can only be changed by changing the parts, while a process can be easily modified by changing the process at any point. A process doesn't have an effect. Instead, it produces *by-products*. When you alter a process, you change the by products. If Bruno were to modify his process of driving to work by driving one more block North before turning West, he'd save a lot of wear and tear on his car.

Here are some examples of common processes we often conceive as things: relationships ... holidays ... waves ... trees... weddings ... personalities ... childhood ... life ... the past ... the present ... the future ... the world ... the mind.

Recognizing that something is a process rather than a thing can have a huge impact on your life.

Chapter Six

Models of the Mind

*Only in imagination does every truth find an
effective and undeniable existence.
Imagination, not invention, is the supreme master of
art, as of life.*

Joseph Conrad

To understand the word *mind* you need a model of it (a
concept) and the characteristics of whatever model you use will be
unconsciously transferred to your own mind. Throughout history
people have used different models to understand the mind. This
limited the mind to the properties of the model. In this way we have
blinded ourselves to many of our natural talents and abilities.

The mind as a storehouse of information

Until the 1950's, the model used
by psychologists to describe the mind
was a library. The mind was pictured
as a vast storehouse of information,
with rows upon rows of volumes, each
containing information about some
area of life. It was believed that each
event of your past was recorded in this library and remembering was
the act of retrieving this stored information.

This model isn't very good. It can't explain why memories
change or how we can remember things that never happened, like
dreams. It can't explain why memories are affected by emotions, or
how memories of two different events can get fused together, so we
seem to have one memory of one event. It can't explain our ideas of
the future, or how a goal can become a source of inspiration. It can't

explain how an inventor can use a mental image of something that has never existed as an aid to develop it.

Although the library model wasn't very good, we used it because we had nothing better.

The mind as a processor of information

After the invention of the computer, scientists began using the computer as a model for the mind. They saw the mind as a device that not only <u>stored</u> information but also <u>processed</u> it.

This model had many of the same deficiencies as the library model did. Both these models treat the mind as a <u>thing</u>, rather than a <u>process</u>.

This affected our understanding of not only how the mind works, but also how life works.

In order to understand how you create your reality you will need a new model of the mind as a process.

This model will describe the mind in terms of its *properties*, opening the door to a new understanding of how it works and of how your life works. This model not only brings it into alignment with our concept of thinking, it also brings it into line with the model of reality developed by the leading scientist of this century.

I'll describe this model beginning in the next chapter.

Chapter Seven

The Mind as Creator

*We are what we think. All that we are arises with
our thoughts. With our thoughts we make our
world.*

The Buddha

Your mind does not simply store
information or process it. Your mind *creates*
information. A concept of the mind as a *creator*
opens up a number of exciting new possibilities.

The mind as creator of information

There's a big difference between data and
information and you need to understand this difference because
information is data *in formation*. When geese fly South for the
winter, they fly "in formation", (usually a "V" shape). When you
write a letter you arrange ink into letters, words and sentences,
creating information from spots of ink. The mind creates
information by organizing sense data into concepts, models and
maps. The same data can be organized many different ways, and *the
context creates the meaning*. To illustrate what I mean I'll give you
some data and organize it a few different ways, creating several
different kinds of information. Here's the data ... 35.

35 by itself has no meaning until placed within a *context*,
which creates the meaning and transforms the data into information.
If I say 35 is my wife's age; that it represents the number of first
cousins I have; or that a friend who sells real estate sold this many
houses last year, I create a series of different contexts. Each context
creates different information from the same data.

This is what the mind does. To illustrate how, take an imaginary walk with me along Vancouver's beautiful English Bay beach.

A walk on the beach

As you walk beside me along the wet sand, your feet make depressions in the sand which fill up with water. Each footprint is an *organizing principle*. It determines the form the water will take as it flows into it. This shape is not the *right* form for the water to take. It is not the *truth* of what the water *should* become. It is not the shape the water *wants* to become. It's just the shape your foot makes in the sand.

When you ask yourself a question you are making a kind of space in your mind, which automatically fills up with data. *The form of the question determines the form of the answer.* This answer will not be *right*. It will not be the *truth*. However (and this is important) *it will seem like the truth to you!* The unconscious process of asking yourself questions and answering them is how you've constructed all the concepts, models and maps in your inner world.

> *Both the content of your mind and the circumstances of your life are the result of the unconscious questions you have been asking yourself*

To change your life and access your personal power you need to begin asking yourself a new kind of question.

How you create your self-image

Suppose that as a child you were not as good at drawing pictures as a classmate, and you asked yourself, *Why can't I draw like Jackie can?* In such a case, your mind might have answered,

32

Drawing takes talent. Jackie has talent and you don't.

If you accepted this answer as true, you'd start to believe you had no talent. Your expectations of the future would be shaped to this self-image. You'd never try to improve and consequently wouldn't improve. Eventually you'd have a coherent set of feelings, thoughts and beliefs supporting this limited self-image. Your *inner* concept would have become your *outer* reality.

This image of yourself would not be the truth. It would have been created in response to the question you'd asked and would no

more reflect a truth about you than the shape of your footprint reflects a truth about water. Both are simply temporary forms created by you which can be changed.

If instead you had asked yourself, *What would I need to do to draw like Jackie?*, you might have gotten the answer, *You need to practice as much as Jackie does.* This answer would lead to a different self-image and to a different life.

The mind as creator of reality

An apple seed transforms soil into wood, leaves, flowers and fruit. The apples eventually produced will be made of material that was originally part of the soil. A tomato seed transforms the <u>same soil</u> into tomatoes. Nothing in the soil decides

to end up as tomatoes, apples or anything else. The magic is in the seeds, which are organizing principles that transform soil into plants, flowers and fruit.

Your mind operates in a similar way. It transforms the data of your senses into a unique set of internal structures (concepts, beliefs, etc.). Your personal reality is simply your recognition of these projected patterns. A question is an organizing principle. It

33

affects the way your mind organizes data and ultimately the reality you create for yourself, as the example of the self-image illustrates.

The focus of your mind can be controlled quite easily when you know how and your senses will select data according to its focus. Questions are *conscious* organizing principles affecting which data feed the *unconscious* organizing principles described earlier. A combination of conscious and unconscious organizing principles ultimately create your personal reality. In a later chapter you will learn a number of other conscious organizing principles giving you great mastery over the information your mind creates and the reality you experience. For now, here's an example of how questions can be used to focus your mind.

Controlling the focus of your mind

To experience just how easily you can control the focus of your mind, take a moment to do the following two exercises.

Exercise 1: controlling your outer awareness

- Look around you and notice things made of metal.
- Now notice things made of wood.
- Now notice things colored orange... green... yellow.
-

Notice how your attention was drawn to different things as you asked yourself each of these questions. Notice how objects or colors that may have been in your field of view were not even noticed until your attention was focused by the questions.

Exercise 2: controlling your inner awareness

- Recall an event that made you feel embarrassed.
- Recall an event that made you feel proud.
- Recall an event that made you feel loved.

Notice how easily your inner awareness focuses on events that fulfill the instructions you give your mind. Paying attention to the unconscious instructions you are giving yourself can give you great insight into how you are influencing the way you are creating your life.

Inner and outer senses

When your mind creates information, it makes use of your *outer* senses to gather data from the physical world and your *inner* senses to gather data from the inner world. Both use the same nerves, so there is a constant interplay between your *conception* of inner reality and your *perception* of outer reality.

Only the present is physical, so your *outer* senses can gather data only from the present. But your inner senses can gather data from any region outside your present location. All data from the past and future, as well as all information contained in concepts, models and maps is gathered through the inner senses. Since you can control the focus of your inner senses, *you have the ability to influence your perception of the physical world*. This is a truly extraordinary ability that should not be underestimated.

Thought forms

All thinking involves the creation of a thought form. Concepts, models and cognitive maps are thought forms, as are memories,

35

wishes and goals. Thought forms can be either visual, auditory, kinesthetic, gustatory or olfactory .

Do you know what a rose smells like?

This question is an organizing principle. It causes your mind to create an *olfactory* thought form.

Can you recognize the sound of a harp being played? A dog howling at the moon? Surf crashing onto a rocky shore? These questions instruct the mind to create *auditory* thought forms using your inner sense of hearing. You imagine holding an ice cube in your hand with your inner sense of *feeling*. You recall the color of your car with your inner sense of *seeing*. You imagine eating a lemon with your inner *gustatory* sense. A musician must perfect the ability to create auditory thought forms. An artist, architect or engineer, visual ones. To consciously create your reality you must cultivate the ability to create thought forms.

Thought forms are known by a multitude of names. Memories, goals, dreams, fears, emotions, worries, ideas, concepts, images, sounds ... all are thought forms. Dreaming, thinking, wondering, worrying, planning, musing, anticipating, fearing, expecting ... all these activities involve *exactly the same process* - the creation of a thought form using the inner senses. The thought forms you create influence the life you experience, and whether you create them consciously or unconsciously is up to you.

> *Remembering the past and anticipating the future*
> *are the same mental process.*

The past and future are nothing but thought forms. Thinking of each involves the exact same action of the mind. Only the organizing principle differs. The more conscious you are of the questions you ask, the more control you have over the thought form created.

36

To conceive the past as a thing is to make the same mistake Bruno does when he conceives the drive to work as a thing. *Remembering* is not a passive process of looking at an unchanging record. It is a *dynamic process* of creating a thought form, the mental equivalent of singing a song. To change a song you need only give it a different tone. You can change your past, your present and your future just as easily.

How your mind creates your reality

Your mind is creating your reality today by creating patterns with the inner senses which it projects onto the outer world. You have been unconsciously creating both internal and external reality since birth. It's now time to wake up and do it consciously. Each time you create a new thought form, you stimulate its appearance in your outer world. This is an exciting process.

Understanding exactly how you create your reality will take time. But accepting a concept of yourself as a person of power creates the possibility of using this power to transform your reality into one containing more of what you want.

Your mind is constantly creating information as easily as nature creates flowers. You can't stop it any more than you can stop plants from appearing in the spring. A tree can't choose which fruit to create but you can choose which questions to ask, just as you can decide which seeds to plant, thereby creating more flowers and less weeds.

We normally think of a flower as a *thing*, but it's actually part of an ongoing *process*. We normally conceive of the world as a thing, but it too is the byproduct of a continuous process, one in which you have been unconsciously involved since birth and which you are now learning to consciously influence.

Whether nature is making flowers, Bruno is making sandwiches or you are asking the questions that stimulate the creation of your dreams and goals, the same creative process is taking place. Simple, isn't it?

Cultivating your personal power

Although the overall creative process is automatic, by practicing a little gardening you can cultivate what you want. Without cultivation your lawn will produce the same weeds that grow next door and your mind will produce a life like that of your neighbours. If you want tomatoes you must plant them. If you want happiness and success you must cultivate it. Only a naive person would sit around wishing for tomato seeds to blow onto his property or expect to achieve his goals and dreams by accident.

 You can choose which concepts to plant in your mind as easily as a gardener chooses which seeds to plant in his garden. A gardener can transform any piece of ground into a botanical masterpiece. You can transform your life the same way.

You begin by looking into your mind to see what concepts are already there, then deciding whether to leave them alone or replace them with others more in line with your purpose and goals.

The concept that exerts the most influence over your life is your *model of the universe*. You call it *reality*. It controls what is possible and impossible, what is real and what is not, what the world contains and the laws under which it operates. This model seems like common sense to you but it's just a model, with limitations built into it. It was created a few hundred years ago and handed down to you.

It has since been replaced by another model, operating under different rules and containing different possibilities. But no one has told you what this change in models means for you.

This is what we'll explore in the next few chapters.

Chapter Eight

Models of the Universe

The universe is beginning to look less like a giant machine and more like a giant thought.

Sir Fred Hoyle

In 1632, Galileo was sent to prison for saying the earth revolved around the sun, a belief contrary to the Church's view of things. He died in prison twelve years later, saying, *The earth does so move.* In 1672 Isaac Newton's model of a sun-centered system was firmly established. In 1994 the Catholic Church finally admitted it had made a mistake in dealing with Galileo.

As stated previously, the model we use to explain something controls what's possible for that thing. In the early years of this century Albert Einstein came up with a new model of the universe which gave a different explanation for the way things work and changed the impossible into the possible. This model has had a profound impact on virtually every aspect of our life, but most people still see themselves through the filter of Newton's model.

Einstein's theory of relativity has changed the way scientists see things, but this change has not made its way into the general consciousness. We continue to view our lives in relation to seventeenth century concepts. A multitude of problems we deal with on a day to day basis disappear overnight when we begin to view ourselves through the lens of Einstein's new physics.

By changing your perspective you gain a new place in the world and a new sense of your personal power. The limitations you have been experiencing disappear and you are able to do things that were once impossible. If you think this sounds too good to be true, take a journey through time with Bruno.

A trip through time

 Imagine that as Bruno is having breakfast one day, he goes outside onto his patio to enjoy a cup of coffee in the fresh air and discovers his back yard has been transported back to the seventeenth century! He finds himself in a country village, surrounded by people who stare at their strangely dressed visitor with a mixture of wonder and fear.

As he begins to speak, they recognize him as a person like themselves. Their curiosity overtakes them when he invites them inside his home.

As they enter his home they become shocked and confused. It is filled with strange devices and unfamiliar materials. Imagine their reaction when he turns on the television! When he pops in a video for them to watch and makes a bowl of popcorn in the microwave, they are astounded! They begin asking Bruno a barrage of questions, trying to understand who this stranger is and what magic he is able to perform.

If he explained that the video tape held images on a magnetic powder would they comprehend? If he explained that his television received waves from a satellite circling the earth, would they understand? If he told them the microwave cooked food by using the same invisible waves, would they believe him? We know that they wouldn't be able to understand his explanations and would be powerless to operate the devices if they stopped working.

But their inability to understand would have nothing to do with intelligence. If they spent some time in the twentieth century they would quickly learn to operate these devices just as Bruno has. No, their inability to comprehend is due entirely to one thing: *They have no conceptual framework with* *which to understand.*

41

Without the concepts of electricity, magnetism, television, satellites and radio waves, they would have no choice but to explain their experience in Bruno's home by inventing explanations which fit their pre-existing mental framework, using concepts they were familiar with.

They might think Bruno a wizard, that the microwave was operated by gods, that there were little people inside the television. If the tv and the microwave stopped working they might think the people had run away or that the gods were displeased.

They might think they'd been possessed by demons, or that Bruno had given them some mysterious poison which made them hallucinate.

These explanations would be wrong. They would involve the invention of artificial mechanisms, false laws and nonexistent entities. But their theories would make sense to the villagers because they would fit their frame of reference and would satisfy their need to explain what they had seen.

When it comes to understanding how your life works, you are in much the same position as these villagers. You've been handed a model of the mind based on concepts from the seventeenth century and told to figure out the way things work.

This model hasn't worked yet, but you keep trying to use it because its the only model you've got. The model you've been given consists of a set of ideas and rules formulated in the seventeenth century which have been largely discarded by the scientific community. But you keep trying to squeeze your life into its limited framework because you don't have another model to work with.

Using this model has blinded you to many of your talents and abilities and forced you into trying to live your life with rules that don't work! Like a villager asked to fix a television, you've been given an impossible task.

Accessing your personal power

Trying to understand your life through an outdated model has forced you to invent nonexistent entities and false mechanisms. It has blinded you to your true creative abilities. Although you have the power to do anything you want, you haven't the tools to access this power. Trying to achieve happiness and success in life has left you confused and frustrated as you experience the same kinds of problems over and over again.

This is all going to change now.

You will soon acquire a new model, based upon modern concepts from the twentieth century. As you begin using this model, your view of yourself will undergo a profound shift. You'll discover new talents and begin to wield a power that has remained dormant within you since you were a child. Your life will be transformed forever.

From Newton's model to Einstein's

In ancient times people believed the world was carried through the universe on the back of a giant turtle. They believed gods in the heavens controlled things on earth. When bad things happened they thought the gods were angry and performed rituals to entice the gods into giving them what they wanted. When confronted with a person who seemed to have a better life, they said this person had been *born under a lucky star*. This explanation fit their model of reality, but made them victims of a metaphysical concept which robbed them of their power.

People in the middle ages believed the universe consisted of a collection of crystal spheres rotating around a stationery earth. Aristotle's statement that a heavy object would fall faster than a light one was accepted as true for sixteen hundred years without anyone testing it! Their belief blinded them to all sorts of evidence to the contrary.

When Galileo proved that both light and heavy objects fall at the same rate, his mathematical formula describing the speed of falling objects marked the first time in history an event was explained by a **mathematical** law rather than a **supernatural** one.

When he published a book saying the earth moved around the sun, he was imprisoned for the last fifteen years of his life. Thirty-two years previously philosopher Giordano Bruno was burned alive at the stake for saying the same thing!

A new model emerges

Other scientists soon enlarged upon Galileo's work, creating a grand theory which explained the world in mathematical terms. This theory, *Newtonian Mechanics,* held sway until 1904, when it was replaced by Einstein's theory.

According to Newton's seventeenth century model, particles called atoms hit each other transferring their energy to one another like a giant game of billiards. The world contains four absolute qualities - space, time, matter and energy. It operates through the action of two absolute principles - the law of *cause and effect* and the principle of *duality.* This states that the physical world and the non-physical world are forever separate with each having no effect on the other. To Newton, time flows like a river from the past to the future. Every present event has a cause in the past which can be known. The future remains unknown.

The theory explained a great number of physical phenomena. People began to regard the past as the cause of the present. They looked upon the future as non-existent, unknowable and without power. The concepts cause and effect and duality came to be considered absolute truths of the world and of our lives! We were once again confusing the model for the thing it represents.

Over time, scientists began to notice more and more phenomena that didn't fit this model. According to Newton, magnetism, electricity and x-rays were impossible but they were clearly real. It became apparent that the model would need to be replaced. In 1904, it was, by Albert Einstein's.

Einstein's model not only explained everything Newton's did, but also these 'impossible' phenomena as well. It also implied a number of new possibilities which in the last hundred years have sparked the invention of radio, television, atomic power, satellites, computers and lasers. All impossible, according to Newton's model.

But the implications of Einstein's model have not yet been incorporated into the way most of us view ourselves. Most of us are still trying to understand ourselves and our worlds with concepts that are a hundred years out of date!

To explain how some people succeed while others fail they invented metaphysical concepts that didn't explain anything. They said winners had *talent*, had *inherited* something from their parents or were *lucky*. No one has ever defined these terms. Is it valid to say someone has talent after she has practiced her craft every day for twenty years? Or to say a person is lucky after trying something a thousand times?

These concepts are simply *ghost terms* invented by a mind trying to apply Newton's model to human behavior. They are no more real than the crystal spheres of antiquity.

What this means to you

The difficulties you experience in life stem from the fact you have been trying to understand your place in the world using inappropriate concepts. Apply a more appropriate model and your difficulties disappear. Simultaneously a world of opportunities opens up to you.

People viewing life through a Newtonian filter look to the past to find a cause for the present. Since the mind always finds what it seeks, they will find things which seem to satisfy the search.

Thinking the future has no power, they will call people who set and achieve their goals *lucky*. Thinking they can't change the past, they won't notice that it's changing constantly.

Unable to see what doesn't fit their model, they'll come to believe they lack the talent to succeed, remaining blind to people all around them who are succeeding with no talent. Believing thoughts have no power, they won't notice that everything physical is created first in the mind. They'll complain they are the victims of bad timing, bad luck or bad parents, unaware that the very concept of a **cause** is a Newtonian idea.

The search for external reasons to explain their lives means they remain blind to the transforming power that exists **right now** inside their own hearts and minds.

It's time to bring our concept of ourselves into the twenty-first century! It's time to create a model of the mind based on the ideas of Einstein rather than Newton. This model will contain different concepts and imply new possibilities. It will give us new eyes to see and new abilities others think are impossible. Using these new abilities will give us the power to transport ourselves from the horse-and-buggy age to the space age.

Chapter Nine

Einstein's Model of the World

The important thing is to not stop questioning. It is enough if one tries merely to comprehend a little of this mystery every day. Never lose a holy curiosity.

Albert Einstein

A model of the mind patterned after Einstein's model of the universe gives the mind many of the attributes modern science now recognizes as real. When I contrast the models of Newton and Einstein it becomes clear that many things we normally accept as features of the mind really reflect aspects of Newton's mechanical model of the universe. Using this model to understand the mind has blinded us to our natural abilities because they didn't fit the model. They were considered impossible. When we adopt Einstein's perspective, these new mental abilities make perfect sense. Some have astounding implications for a new empowering view of ourselves.

Contrasting Newton's model and Einstein's

In Newton's model the world was considered to operate like a giant billiard game. Physical particles (*atoms*) moved because of *forces*. Interactions involving particles were called *events*.

47

The non-physical (*spiritual)* world was separate from the physical and had no effect on it.

Time was *absolute,* running like a river from the past to the future.

Every event had an *absolute cause* in the past, and an absolute *effect* in the future.

Einstein's model interprets the world in a very different way. The qualities of Einstein's model are quite different from those of Newton's and lead to interpretations so different they were originally considered impossible. They have since been proven correct. In fact, Einstein's model is the most verified scientific theory of all time.

Matter, energy, probability and the quantum

In Einstein's model atoms are not physical and energy is not a force. Instead, matter and energy are two sides of the same coin, called a *quantum*, which can appear to be a physical *particle* or a wave of *energy* depending on how we look at it. The actions of these particle/wave packets are *not* absolute. They are described in terms of *probability*. Matter can become energy. Energy can become matter. The physical and non-physical are not separate. Indeed, every event is a combination of the physical and the non physical.

Uncertainty and causality

Single events are not predictable but *patterns of events* are. We can predict how many automobile accidents will occur on a given weekend or how many atoms of uranium will decay in a certain period of time, but we can't predict which automobiles or which atoms will be involved. For any single event no definite cause can be found. The cause for an event can even be non physical!

Fields and action at a distance

The new theory includes the concept of a *field*. A magnetic field influences a compass needle and a planet's gravitational field influences a comet's flight. Every particle in the universe affects every other. As the Chinese say, "When a butterfly beats its wings the stars move."

Relativity and the lack of absolutes

There are no absolutes. Speed, time, distance, mass, location and direction are relative. All measurements depend upon the *frame of reference*, and there is *no* absolute frame of reference. A person in an elevator can't tell whether the elevator is standing still on earth or accelerating through space. Measurements made in one frame of reference tell you nothing about conditions in another frame of reference.

The connection of the physical and the spiritual

Gravity affects matter. Physical properties change according to an object's speed. Both matter and energy are influenced by fields. The non-physical affects the physical. The idea of separation is given up forever.

Virtual particles

When matter is created from energy, particles appear from a cloud of *possible* particles like raindrops forming out of a cloud. Particles which might have been created but weren't are called *virtual particles*. These are non-physical entities which exert a measurable influence on the physical particles.

Like a flock of sheep leaving a pen, the one first through the gate is the *actual* leader. But the entire population are *virtual* leaders. The ones nearest the gate have the *highest probability* of being first and the behavior of all affects the eventual outcome. After one has made it through the gate we will know the *actual* result and will never be able to say exactly *why* this result occurred.

49

Past, present and future

According to Einstein's theory, there is nothing to distinguish past from future. It depends on the frame of reference. The same event could be in the past, present or future. The cause for a present event might even be in the future! In Einstein's universe *virtual future events* influence the present as much as past events!

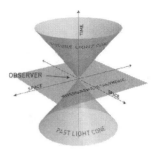

Space-time, wormholes and multiple universes

Like matter and energy, space and time are also two sides of the same coin, which Einstein called *space-time*. The laws of space and the laws of time mirror each other. Time travel is as possible as space travel.

Gravity is not a force. It is a bending of space-time. When strong enough, the bending can create a hole in the physical universe called a *black hole*. Something drawn into it is sucked out of space and *travels through time*, where it emerges from a *white hole* in a different space-time location! Because neither time nor distance has any absolute meaning, the particle is in *two locations at once*. These separate space-time locations are connected by a *wormhole,* like a tunnel connects two points on opposite sides of a river.

One implication of this new conceptual framework is that there are a multitude of *virtual worlds*, giving a place and a time for every possible event to occur. When flipping a coin in Einstein's world, it lands *both* heads *and* tails, but each event occurs in its own world!

To a person in world A, the coin lands *heads* and tails is a virtual event that never materialized. A person in world B will see the coin land *tails*. To this person, *heads* is a possibility that never materialized. All worlds are connected by wormholes. What is

50

physical in one world is *non-physical* in another. The border between the virtual and the real is a matter of perspective.

How can you tell which universe you are in? you may ask.

According to modern physics, you can't! We are all trapped inside our own private frame of reference. No matter how much evidence we gather, we can never know for certain what's happening in someone else's world.

But, what is the **real** truth? you might ask.

However in Einstein's world the question is invalid. Absolute truth is a Newtonian concept. It has been discarded. In Einstein's universe it makes no more sense to ask about *absolute* truth than to ask, "How many angels can *really* dance on the head of a pin?"

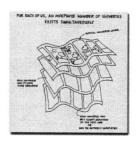

No matter what we believe, we will never be able to prove it outside our own frame of reference. When we change the frame of reference the meaning of events shifts to line up with our new point of view. Since everything is a matter of perspective, whatever evidence you gather will support what you choose to accept. There is no such thing as *the* truth, only *your* truth.

Applying Einstein's model to your life

Modern physics provides us with a new model we can apply to our life, giving us new insight into how we create recurring *patterns* of events and implying new abilities that were previously considered impossible.

There are many worlds. We each create our own. Your frame of reference is your choice. You are free to choose the laws of your world. You are free to choose the meaning of every event. Whether anything is positive or negative is a matter of perspective. You are free to choose the overall pattern of your life and choose what your life will ultimately mean.

Your physical present sits between a spectrum of virtual pasts and virtual futures. It is connected equally to the past and the future.

Your past is not physical. It is a thought form. Your future is another thought form. Both contain numerous possibilities connected to your present through the medium of your mind Both affect your present as any thought form does.

Your mind has a counterpart to memory which operates in the future. You are able to gather information from the future as easily as from the past.

You have the power to transform your past and to influence which possible future becomes real. A clear concept of your chosen future as an already existing (virtual) reality, gives you the opportunity to connect with it, providing the information you need to help it materialize in your physical present.

You can give up the struggle of trying to live according to someone else's beliefs and choose instead the boundaries of your own world.

By coupling a new conceptual framework with a new belief in your personal power, you transport yourself from the seventeenth century into the twenty-first!

A note to the reader

At this point I want you to pause in your reading of this material. I want to summarize what we have covered so far so you don't miss the importance of it.

 We began this discussion with reference to the idea that down through history, certain people -- magicians, like Merlin -- possessed a secret power to make things happen. They could make things appear out of nothing. They could make things disappear. They could transform something of no value to something of great value -- turn 'lead' into 'gold'.

We then said that the key to this power lies is your thoughts. Your thoughts are the magic elixir that confers this power on you.

Next we explained what a thought is. It is an internal model that represents reality.

Then we explained that we get lost in these models, confusing them for reality itself. Remember the example of the two people meeting the dog in the park? Each experienced the dog in a completely different way. But both thought their experience was because of the dog -- not their internal concept of the dog. They each confused their internal model with reality itself -- they confused *inner* reality with *outer* reality. This is the great trap we all get caught in.

Next we discussed the idea that what we think of the mind itself is a model -- it is not reality either!

And this model is based on what we think is possible in the world. If something is impossible in the world, then it must be impossible for us.

However, what we think of as the world is just another model -- one that was invented in the seventeenth century -- before people new what a germ or an atom or light or gravity was.

In this model, everything happens because of a cause, and the cause is always in the past. You can't change the past because it's already happened.

You can't know the future because it hasn't happened yet.

Things are physical. Ideas, which are non-physical, have no effect on what's 'real'.

Because we accepted this **model** of the world as **reality**, we assumed that these aspects of the model were true for us as well, because we are physical beings.

However, in the 20th century, Einstein came up with a new model -- one that says the physical and the non-physical **are** connected; that the past and the future are both **equally real**; that the cause for something can be **in the future**; that there are an infinite number of possible universes -- all equally real; that **wormholes** allow information and energy to travel instantly from one place in space or in time to another; that **virtual realities** have a real influence.

 In the coming chapters we will create a new model of the mind based on Einstein's model of the universe. When we begin to apply this new model to our lives, we will realize that we have the power to create the life we want.

We will be able to make opportunities appear as if by magic. We will be able to make 'mistakes' disappear as if they never happened.

We will no longer accept limitations because we were born with no 'talent', because we realize that 'talent' is a Newtonian concept. We now have the ability to create new talents for ourselves.

No longer will we look upon people who live extraordinary lives   as people who are 'lucky' because we will know how to create our own luck.

I welcome you to your new magical ability to create the life of your choice.

Chapter Ten

A New Model of the Mind

*The metaphor is one of man's most fruitful
potentialities. Its efficacy verges on magic, a tool
for creation which God forgot inside one of His
creatures when He made him.*

Jose Ortega y Gasset

The search for truth, whether in science or religion, is always a search for simplicity. An overly complex explanation defeats understanding. A simple one aids it. It's a basic scientific principle that if two theories compete to explain the same phenomena, the simpler one is better.

The history of science contains lots of examples of a simple theory replacing a complex one. People in the middle ages believed the stars moved around a stationary earth. They also believed the circle was the perfect curve. This meant the planets must move around the earth in perfect circles. Yet observations clearly showed that some stars (*planets*) moved in strange ways.

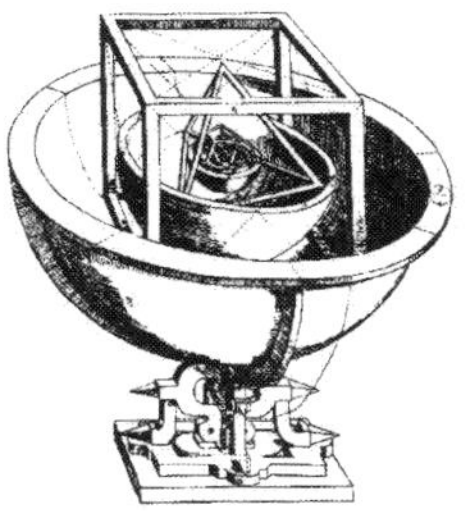

To align their observations with their beliefs, astronomers constructed a complex model of planetary motion consisting of numerous wheels, within wheels, within wheels. The model did manage to duplicate the motion of the planets but it sacrificed simplicity.

When they gave up the belief in 'perfect' circular motion and the belief in the earth as the centre of everything, they realized planets moved in ellipses around the sun.

55

Complexity vanished and a simple model of planetary motion was born.

A similar situation occurred in the early years of this century. Scientists had several competing theories to explain the phenomena of x-rays, electromagnetism, and the photo-electric effect. Einstein's concept of the *quantum* brought these seemingly unrelated phenomena into one simplified system. Like any new 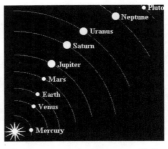 theory, Einstein's predicted things which at first seemed impossible but which ultimately proved valid. It has since led to scores of new discoveries and inventions.

The wide variety of processes taking place in the mind appear complex. The connection between our thinking and the world seems mysterious. But it doesn't have to be. Borrowing a few concepts from Einstein we can build a model of consciousness that greatly simplifies an inner world which until now has seemed mysterious.

Our model implies things previously considered impossible. But these ideas will suddenly seem obvious as we understand, perhaps for the first time, the relationship between our inner and outer worlds.

Our new model places the creation of your personal reality under your direct influence. No longer will you feel victimized by forces you can't control or at the mercy of a past you can't change. No longer will you feel intimidated by a future that appears frightening. With this new model you'll be able to cultivate a powerful new personality, to transform negative emotions and stressful situations into positive ones. You'll realize that the power to create positive circumstances lies within your grasp.

Changing some of your long-standing internal programming will take work, certainly, but the effort needed to root out your fears, false beliefs and limiting self-concept will pay off many times over as you enjoy a new found confidence and a new self-image.

Building the model

Our model will consist of the following concepts and definitions:

- inner space-time
- inner and outer awareness
- the now point
- virtual events

It will also include a new model of the ***imagination*** and a further refinement in our description of the process of ***thinking***.

In this chapter, we'll use these concepts and definitions to describe the operation of the mind in a dramatically new way. In the next we'll explore some exciting implications of this new model.

Inner space-time (Figure 1)

The first concept in our model is *inner space-time*. This is an inner, mental landscape, a large cognitive map that provides a place for every past, present and future possibility. It also contains all concepts and mental models. Just as a map of your neighbourhood fits into a larger map of the world, all cognitive maps of various parts of your life fit into the overall map called inner spacetime.

If you imagine a map of inner space-time with the future at the top and the past at the bottom, the equator would represent the *present*, the border between past and future.

Your world line

Your world line traces the path you have taken through time. It connects the *real* events of your past, strung together like a string of pearls. On a map of inner spacetime, your world line looks like a railroad track, passing through various locations.

The now point

This is where your world line touches the boundary between the past and the future. This is the physical present. This is where your body is.

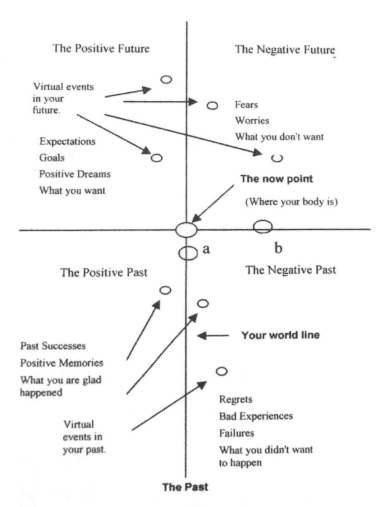

The Future

The Positive Future   The Negative Future

Virtual events
in your
future.

                 Fears
                 Worries

                 What you don't want

Expectations
Goals
Positive Dreams
What you want

The now point

(Where your body is)

a   b

The Positive Past   The Negative Past

Past Successes
Positive Memories
What you are glad
happened

Your world line

Virtual
events in
your past.

Regrets
Bad Experiences
Failures
What you didn't want
to happen

The Past

A Map of Inner Space Time
Figure 1

If you were in a car traveling through the countryside, the route you actually drove would be your world line. The now point would be the car you were sitting in. You would see the landscape whizzing by the window as you sat driving. You would be able to see a little way into the future (ahead of you), a little way into the past (behind you) and a little way into the countryside alongside the road. If you were driving alongside a river, you might be able to see a car on the other side of the river. This other car would be a virtual present for you. It represents a possibility that could have happened, if you had taken that route.

Virtual events and real events

Virtual events are mental events. *Past* virtual events which were real in the past are points on your route that you passed through. (This is 'a' in Figure 1) Past virtual events which *might* have happened but didn't, lie to the right or left of your world line. These are places you could have driven through but did not.

Future virtual events lie in the future. If we extend your world line into the future, we create a line pointing straight ahead, virtual future events which are highly probable lie close to this track. The farther we go to the left or right, the less probable are the future virtual events.

Present virtual events (This is 'b' in Figure 1) are events which might be happening now that we aren't certain of because they lie outside the range of our physical senses. They lie over the horizon to the left or right of the train.

If we arbitrarily consider the *left* side of our map to represent the *positive* and the *right* side *negative*, then positive past virtual events Things we wish had happened) lie to the southwest. Positive future virtual events (Things we'd like to happen) lie to the northwest. Negative past virtual events (Things we're glad didn't happen) lie to the southeast. Negative future virtual events lie to the northeast.

You can think of future virtual events this way: If you flip a coin a minute from now, the chances of it landing heads or tails are equal. Both possibilities exist as virtual events in your future. They

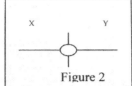

Figure 2

could be represented as points on your map an equal distance to the left or right of the extension of your world line. Let's call heads X and tails Y. (Figure 2)

If the coin lands heads, X becomes the now point. Y remains a virtual event (*a parallel present*) lying off to one side. It never becomes a real event. (Figure 3)

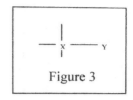

Figure 3

As your car (the now point) moves into the future, it crosses X, which moves into the past as a point on your world line. It traces a path from the *possible future*, through the *now point*, into the *past*.

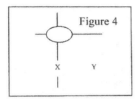

Figure 4

Y, on the other hand, never becomes part of the world line. It traces a path from the *possible future*, through a *parallel present*, into the *virtual past*. It remains forever a possible event that never materialized. It's like a town through which your car might have passed, but didn't. (Fig. 4)

For a person in the next town unaware of how the coin has landed, both X and Y remain virtual events until something provides her with information of what actually took place. This information determines which event becomes real for her.

This situation is like what would happen if you were planning a trip and couldn't decide which of two towns to visit. A friend back home wouldn't know where you were on a given day until you called to tell her what you'd decided. Until then she'd be left with two possibilities to think about and not know which one was real. When you call and tell her that you decided to visit town "A", her reality shifts.

Since we each have knowledge others lack, some events which are real for someone else are virtual for you, and visa-versa. In this way each of us experiences a unique combination of real and virtual events.

Your personal reality is unique

The fact that each person's inner reality is unique causes nearly all our interpersonal strife and confusion. Our common language makes it seem that we share a common world, when in fact we each experience a unique arrangement of real and virtual events and each confuse *beliefs* about the world with **knowledge** about it.

If I <u>believe</u> something to be true I will act as though it <u>is</u> true. You may put things together quite differently. In this way our models of the world will diverge as we each construct a unique reality. (I remind you here of the couple encountering the dog in the park.)

Although your world clearly shares certain aspects of reality with mine, it is quite different from my world. (This idea has important implications that we'll explore in the following chapters.)

For each of us, inner space-time contains lots of virtual events like Y. Some bear a close relationship to events that *were* real, or may *become* real. Others are quite different. But *whether real or virtual, all events provide us with equal amounts of information.*

All events, real or virtual, provide us with equal amounts of information

---

How problems are created

We can imagine a future that's highly likely or one that's virtually impossible. When we imagine a past event that didn't happen, our mind fills with information so similar to when we think of an event that did, we get confused.

If we expect a future that doesn't happen and feel badly because we believed it <u>would</u> we are making a basic (and very common) mistake. This causes great strife in our relationships if we

62

criticize our partner for not behaving the way we *believe* he or she
should. The problem is completely artificial. It arises from
confusing a *conception* of a virtual reality with a *perception* of an
actual one.

The virtual past and the real past

Events from history exist in inner space-time just like events
from fiction. The scene in *Casablanca* in which Humphrey Bogart
first sees Ingrid Bergman sitting in Rick's cafe, is as real for us as
the scene of Neil Armstrong's first step onto the moon. For this
reason fictional characters can serve effectively as role models. My
son Graham used to love to run around the house dressed as
Batman, someone as real to him as anyone he saw on the nightly
news.

*The key to developing your personal power is learning to use the
virtual past and the virtual future as a sources of information.*

Future virtual events provide us with as much information as
real past events. This is the secret power of goal-setting. If we wish
to experience a positive future and ask ourselves, *What can I do to
help bring this situation about?* our imagination provides us with
the answer.

If we wish to avoid a negative future and ask ourselves, *How
can I avoid this situation?* our mind again provides answers. We
will be fully exploring the implications of this process in a later
chapter.

The key to using the virtual past and the virtual future as a
source of information depends on new models of the imagination
and of the awareness. This is what we'll cover next.

The awareness

Your awareness is the *focus of your attention.* It determines the
content of your conscious mind. To put it another way, of all the

63

thoughts you <u>could</u> be thinking at the moment, the one you <u>are</u> thinking is due to the focus of your attention. In other words, what you are <u>conscious</u> of at any time depends on the focus of your attention.

The structure of the awareness

Your awareness has two components ... *outer awareness* and inner *awareness*, summarized as *Ao* and *Ai*.

Your *outer* awareness is focused in the *present*. It collects outer sense data from the physical world through your outer senses.

Your *inner* awareness exists *outside* the present in some area of inner spacetime. It might be focused in the past, the future or in some parallel present. It collects inner sense data through your inner senses.

At any moment your conscious mind contains a *combination* of inner and outer sense data. You can focus on the feelings in your left foot, the sounds in your room, the memory of a friend's face or tonight's dinner party. You can change the focus of your attention easily by deciding to do so. An unlimited amount of inner and outer data is always available to your conscious mind but doesn't become part of it until you focus your attention on it.

> *The focus of your attention is (potentially) under your direct, conscious control.*

The contents of the awareness can be summarized in the following formula.

$A=As+Ai$

Your inner awareness and outer awareness are linked together like a pair of telephones. When you talk with a friend on the phone, your phone and hers are doing exactly the same thing... gathering data. The connection carries the information back

and forth between your two locations.

The connection between your two phones is a telephone wire. The connection between your inner and your outer awareness is your imagination.

The Imagination

Like the telephone wire, your imagination has two ends. One is connected to your outer awareness. The other to your inner awareness. Like the telephone wire your imagination carries information collected by your inner awareness into the present where you become conscious of it as you focus your attention on it.

The pipeline of the Imagination (Figure 5)

As your inner awareness moves through *inner space-time* it draws in sense data from various areas of the virtual past, virtual present or virtual future through your inner senses, like a vacuum

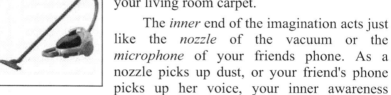

cleaner picks up dust from different areas of your living room carpet.

The *inner* end of the imagination acts just like the *nozzle* of the vacuum or the *microphone* of your friends phone. As a nozzle picks up dust, or your friend's phone picks up her voice, your inner awareness gathers information and transmits it to you in the present.

All thinking is the processing of information from outside your present space-time location.

As your inner awareness moves through inner spacetime drawing in sense data through your inner senses, it acts like your friends cel phone picking up her voice as she moves around the house or around the country.

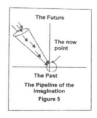

The Future

The now point

The Past

The Pipeline of the Imagination
Figure 5

Inner data are processed with the *same nerves* used to process outer data from the physical world. This is a vitally important point. It reveals both the source of your problems and the key to your power.

The screen of your mind

In your mind is a kind of inner television screen onto which your thoughts are projected. Just as the information on your television screen originates outside the set and comes into it through a cable, when you imagine something, the information comes from outside the now point and comes into your mind through the pipeline of your imagination.

> *Your imagination connects the present to all past, present and future virtual realities*

Inner visual information (mental pictures) travel through the pipeline of your imagination and are projected onto the screen of the mind. Because thinking uses all five inner senses, some thoughts are experienced as images while others are experienced as sounds, tastes, smells or feelings.

This new model of the mind will be the key to discovering and using a host of new talents and abilities you have been unaware of until now.

A new definition of thinking

In chapter two we defined thinking as constructing models of reality. Now that we know the material for constructing these models comes from outside the present we can expand upon this definition.

Thinking is a behavior. It is the process of drawing sense data from inner space-time into the present. The wide variety of confusing labels we have assigned to this behavior are due to the misconception that thoughts of the past and thoughts of the future are different processes. They are not. They are the same process.

Like the "wheels within wheels" model of antiquity, this misconception has made a simple process appear mysterious and overly complex.

In remembering a past event or planning a future one, you are performing exactly the same operation. Your inner awareness *gathers* data. Your imagination *channels* it into the present. Your mind *organizes* it into patterns of information. The various labels applied to different kinds of thinking and the various effects ascribed to them are due purely to differences of belief.

Both *worrying* and *planning* for example, use data from the negative future. A worrier believes the negative possibility is unavoidable. This belief creates feelings of fear and *powerlessness*. A planner believes ways can be found to either avoid the negative event or minimize its effect. This leads to feelings of *confidence and power*.

Some Examples of the Thinking Process

Here are some examples of the very same process to which we have assigned a variety of different and confusing names.

Remembering

Drawing inner sense data from a past that was real into the present.

Regretting

Drawing inner sense data from the positive virtual past into the present, feeling sad that the positive event didn't happen.

Rejoicing

Drawing inner sense data from the negative virtual past into the present, feeling good that the negative event didn't happen.

Worrying

Drawing inner sense data from the negative future into the present, believing it to be unavoidable and feeling afraid of it.

Goal-setting

Drawing inner sense data from the positive future into the present, believing it will happen and feeling positive about it.

The good news

In every case, the process of gathering the data is exactly the same. The different effects are due to differences in meaning due to one's personal beliefs.

The good news is that when we understand the process of information-gathering and the process of meaning-formation we can influence both processes, leading to different effects. We can change our mental focus. We can ask different questions. Like Bruno choosing a different route to work, our choices create effects that can be consciously controlled.

Learning to cultivate more conscious control over these twin aspects of our mind's operation is the subject of the second half of the book. In later chapters we will explore how asking ourselves a different kind of question leads to increasing personal power and conscious choice.

Remembering, regretting, worrying, planning, problem-solving, goal-setting, fearing, wondering, daydreaming, imagining, hallucinating and fantasizing are different names given to exactly the same process. The apparent differences arise from of the way the inner data is organized into different meanings. As long as the organizing principles remain unconscious, we have no power over what data is collected or the meaning given to it. The trick is to become conscious of what's going on internally. The more aware we are the more power and control we have.

How you create problems for yourself

Your personal reality at any moment is made up of a *combination* of physical and non-physical sense data. Remain unaware of this mixture and you'll misinterpret both inner events and outer events. This creates havoc with your emotions. It interferes with your reasoning. It influences your behavior. Remaining unconscious of the interplay of inner and outer sense data is the most common mistake each of us makes and is the source of most of our problems.

To remain unaware of this mixture of inner and outer sense data makes us victims of our imagination as our inner awareness whips about through a spectrum of inner space-time realities. We feel like a victim of circumstances when we are really a victim of our own lack of awareness and control.

To control our emotions and develop our personal power we need to do two things: control the region of inner space-time from which our inner awareness is drawing data and control the meaning we give to it. This requires considerable insight and training. As we gain control over our imagination and inner awareness we become increasingly able to choose our thoughts, our feelings, our behavior and ultimately the makeup of our reality.

69

Training the imagination and the awareness

Without training your inner awareness will be constantly moving between the future and the past, the positive and the negative, collecting inner sense data and drawing it into the present like a cosmic vacuum cleaner gone wild. With no control over the movement of our inner awareness we become bound by fear, worry and negative emotions.

With training, the imagination and the inner awareness can be made to deliver specific data from a specific region of inner space-time.

If asked, *What do you know about ancient Greece?* your awareness takes in several centuries of time in one shot. If asked, *What does a hair on a fly's leg look like?* it focuses in tightly on a microscopic area. To imagine one entire cycle of the orbit of Haley's comet your inner sense of time speeds up. You see the entire seventy-six year cycle in a second.

Neither time nor distance has any meaning in inner space-time. Your imagination is of infinitely variable length. Your inner awareness moves with infinite speed. You can recall an event from twenty-five years ago as easily as one from twenty-five minutes ago. You can imagine what life might have been like a thousand years ago or might be like a thousand years in the future.

> *The degree of control you exercise over your inner awareness determines your degree of personal power*

Your awareness can be trained to filter <u>in</u> or filter <u>out</u> specific kinds of sense data for transport into the now point. This is the secret power of meditation, goal-setting, problem solving, invention and every creative or artistic endeavor. It involves learning to still your mind and focus your attention. Training yourself to do this is one of the most important keys to developing your personal power. It's something we'll cover more completely in later chapters.

For now simply try to grasp the huge range of motion and potential content of your inner awareness. Try to get a sense of the power and resources available to you when you learn to control this aspect of your being. I think you'll agree there's more to the workings of your imagination than you might have considered before.

Properties of the imagination and inner awareness

To summarize, these are the properties of the imagination and the inner awareness.

- The imagination is always working.
- The imagination uses all five inner senses.
- The imagination operates in all regions of inner space-time.
- The imagination uses the same nerves as the outer senses.
- The inner awareness can be expanded or focused.
- The inner awareness can filter in or out specific sense data.
- The inner awareness moves with infinite speed.
- The inner awareness and the imagination can be trained.

This is our new model of the mind. In the next chapter we'll explore some exciting implications of this new way of looking at the mind's operation.

Part Two

Using Your Hidden Power

"At any moment in time
your confidence, courage
and success are only
one thought away."

Chapter Eleven

What the New Model Means to You

> *Man is not the creature of circumstances.*
> *Circumstances are the creatures of men.*
>
> Benjamin Disraeli

This chapter marks a transition between the first half of the book and the second. It also marks a transition between your life as it *was* and your life as it *will be*.

In the last chapter we created a new model which gave us a new way of describing how your mind operates and a new way of understanding how your life works.

In this chapter I'll look at some implications of this model and preview the second half of the book, which contains practical techniques for *using* the model to gain greater control over both your inner and your outer life.

In applying this information you'll be using some abilities you have been unaware of until now. As you use these you will naturally develop greater insight, increased self-confidence and more personal power.

You'll experience steadily increasing control over your feelings, your emotions, your imagination and your behavior. This will lead ultimately to increased control over the external conditions of your life.

This will take effort of course. And some aspects of the process may not be easy. But these new concepts and techniques will provide the tools to create your own road map to the future of your choice as well as make your journey more rewarding.

The connection between
internal and external reality

Our new model firmly establishes the connection between internal and external reality. We each experience the automatic projection of our unconscious mental processes. In simple terms, external reality is the unconscious projection of our inner world.

Our mind is engaged in a never-ending stream of creative manifestation, constantly projecting our inner reality outward like a song we are forever singing. When we learn to "sing a different tune" we can eliminate certain negative aspects of our reality and increase the positive. As we gain control over our inner being, our outer circumstances undergo a shift.

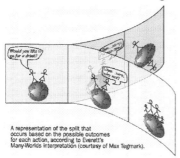

A representation of the split that occurs based on the possible outcomes for each action, according to Everett's Many-Worlds Interpretation (courtesy of Max Tegmark).

Both the past and the future are nothing but concepts, They can be changed in a heartbeat. Contrary to what we have previously believed, we are not victims of a past over which we have no control. The past can be changed. And the future we expect will not necessarily manifest, no matter how much we expect it to. Both the past and the future are simply thought forms and we are their creator!

The unconscious aspects of our personality are as subtle as our posture or voice tone. Even to become aware of them is a great achievement. Learning to alter them is not an easy process. But the rewards are worth the effort.

The present is your point of power

Since the past and future are nothing but thought forms, all of inner space-time is being continually re-created by us in the present moment. The now point connects the past and the future and is the point at which the mental becomes physical. The present moment is the only place you can exercise your power and where your power is manifest. But since you are always in the present, your power is always available to you.

At any moment in time, your power is only one thought away.

Your thinking connects the physical and the non physical

Thinking is processing *inner* sense data. Perceiving is processing *outer* sense data. At any moment, your personal reality is a combination of *both* virtual events and real events. The main difficulty we face in life is sorting the physical from the non-physical. The spiritual and the physical are connected. And you are the connection between them.

The influence of the non physical

Because both inner and outer sense data are processed in a similar way each event has a similar effect on you whether the event is real or virtual. The emotions triggered by a virtual event are as real as those triggered by a real one. When we mistake a rope for a snake, the fear is real even though the snake is imaginary.

Both past and the future events affect us in a similar way. If we're afraid of dogs, we feel the fear in the present whether we are remembering a past encounter or anticipating a future one.

A goal can empower us today, even though it's manifestation is years away

A strong expectation about achieving a goal can empower us today even though the physical manifestation of the goal itself may be years away.

Learning to use the power of the non-physical involves working with both the past and the future, decreasing the negative effects and increasing the positive effects of each.

Decreasing the negative effect of the past

Memory is not a recording of the past. It is a re-creation of it in the present. The nature of memory is the same as worrying, goal-setting, regretting, rejoicing, hoping, fearing or anticipating. The only difference is the *area* of inner space-time from which the imagination draws its data and the *meaning* given to it

When we speak, our vocal chords re-create the same patterns over and over again and someone listening in the next room might mistake the sound of our voice for a tape recording of it. The same is true for remembering, but because the process is unconscious we don't notice what's taking place during remembering. We think we're playing a recording of a past event when we're really creating something new. This misconception robs us of our power. It makes us feel bound by a past we think can't be changed. But the past can be changed in a heartbeat and when we change it, we change its effect on us.

Our voice will sound the same tomorrow as it did yesterday unless we change it. Our memories of yesterday will be repeated tomorrow unless we change the way we think about things. Repeated use of the same limiting concepts over and over again is the real cause of fear, procrastination and worry, and the real cause of our stress, tension and disease.

Past events we believe were negative will continue to cause us pain until we change them. To unlock our personal power we must realize that the emotions we feel when thinking of the past are not due to what happened but to the *meaning* we have given it. We will cover changing the past in chapters 13 and 16.

Changing a concept changes both the past and the future

Increasing the positive effect of the past

Each time you recall a past success you feel good. Developing the habit of dwelling on past successes increases your positive feelings **in the present** and changes your attitude about the future. When we transform past events from negative to positive, we shift our attitudes, beliefs and expectations in a positive direction. Creating a concept of a positive future stimulates the power to create it. We cover this in chapters 17 to 20.

Decreasing the negative effect of the future

Fear, procrastination and worry begin as negative concepts of the future which trigger negative emotions. This leads to tension in your body, stress in your relationships and problems in your world. Since the same concepts are used in both past and future, transforming a negative past event into a positive one automatically decreases the amount of negative energy in the past **and** the future.

Worry is your negative imagination using you. Goal-setting is you using your positive imagination. In each case your imagination draws inner data from the future into the present. But in the one case, the data causes problems. In the other it creates a solution. We cover this in detail in chapters 18 and 20.

Increasing the positive effect of the future

The key to eliminating worry and using the future to your advantage is to cultivate a positive **concept** of it coupled with a positive **belief** in your ability to create what you want.

Achieving a goal is as simple as walking to the store to buy a loaf of bread. Applying this skill to every aspect of your life is something only a handful of people master. Those who do are successful in every area of life.

Chapter 19 gives detailed instructions for creating a blueprint for the life of your choice and explains how to design plans to create it. This involves drawing from the future the information you need to overcome obstacles and solve problems. This process moves you from being a victim of the future to the master of it.

Eliminating negative experiences from your life

Events are only negative if we define them that way. The following chapters contain specific techniques for changing the way you define things, giving you more control over the contents of your mind and the contents of your life. Changing the definitions you use eliminates negative conditions and produces increasing confidence, power and self-esteem. Eliminating negative experiences frees our creative spirit and liberates our energy.

Eliminating negative emotions

All negative emotions arise from differences between our **inner** awareness and our **outer** awareness, between what we expect and what we get. If we get less than expected we feel angry, sad, frustrated, confused or depressed - exactly which emotion we feel depends on our beliefs. By designing a new belief system, we not only eliminate negative emotions, we gain the power to create a new set of positive ones. Specific techniques for doing this are covered in chapter 15.

Using your imagination as a creative force

You either become conscious of what your imagination is doing and learn to direct it or you remain unconscious, allowing it to create what you don't want. When you understand worry, you'll see that the same process can help you achieve your goals, eliminate your fears and develop your personal power. We cover this in chapter 20.

The importance of mental gardening

Cultivating your personality is like clearing the rocks and weeds from a piece of property and transforming it into a garden. The work is not complicated. It just takes planning and effort. The second half of the book provides the plan. Providing the effort is up to you.

The following chapters contain specific instructions for consciously cultivating your skills in all these areas...

- Working with your attitudes and beliefs
- Developing an empowering self-image
- Healing your past wounds
- Transforming negative events into positive ones
- Erasing negative emotions
- Cultivating positive emotions
- Drafting a blueprint of your chosen future
- Forming a plan to create it.
- Building motivation.
- Taking action.

But it will be up to you to become actively involved in creating the life you want - to systematically cultivate this piece of property you have inherited. This book can show you *what* to do and *how* to do it. But you must convince yourself *why* doing it is important. Waiting for someone else to motivate you is a loser's attitude. You must provide your own motivation. You'll learn how in chapter 20.

A new model of consciousness

If the old models of the mind are inappropriate what might be a better model? If thinking of the mind as a library or a computer limits us, what model can we use that brings our understanding of consciousness into the twenty-first century?

Star Trek fans will be pleased to know that the best one I have found is to begin thinking of the mind as a time machine. We'll explore this model in the next chapter.

Chapter Twelve
Your mind contains a time machine

The world would open up and both the past and the future would be visible to our eyes.

Pierre Laplace

Einstein is reported to have said that ***the laws of space and the laws of time mirror each other***. Do the laws of the inner world mirror those of the outer world? Let's examine them and see.

One characteristic of the **outer** world is that data moves through it from one point to another. Some systems for transporting data are sound waves, radio waves, light waves and wires like television cables and telephone lines. The data carried by each is transformed into information by the receiving device whether an eye, an ear, a television or a telephone. Is the same true of the **inner** world?

We've already said that the imagination transports data from one area of inner space-time to another. Does this mean the mind functions like a kind of time machine?

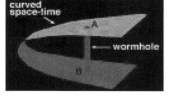

According to Einstein's theory of relativity the speed of light is a limiting speed in the physical world. If something were to travel faster than this it would leave space and begin traveling through time. It would exist in two places at once with the separate locations connected by a wormhole,

81

which is a tunnel connecting the two separate space-time locations. Does the same model fit the non-physical world?

We've already said the awareness moves with infinite speed and is split into two parts, one outer and one inner. Does this mean the imagination is a wormhole connecting two space-time locations, conveying information between them?

When you think of the past or the future, isn't your awareness in two places at once? When you are daydreaming, isn't your mind somewhere else? When worrying, aren't you reacting to where your inner awareness is? When planning a dinner party, isn't part of your mind in the present and part in the future?

These are interesting questions, aren't they?

I believe modern scientific descriptions of the quantum mechanical universe provide an excellent metaphor to understand how the mind operates in inner space-time.

Consider the following example.

Bruno takes a train trip

Inner space-time can be visualized as a map, like that of a country. On such a map a person's world line would be like a train track connecting a series of towns dotted throughout the country. Let's imagine Bruno is a passenger on a train traveling along just such a track, from a town in the South to another in the North.. What potential information would such a model provide for us?

First of all, Bruno's position at any moment is easy to identify...he's on the train...a physical thing existing in the present. The train is his **now point**. Towns through which he'd already passed would be **points on his world line**. Towns farther along would be **probable future events**. Towns through which the train didn't pass would be **virtual events**. They represent possible places he might have visited but didn't.

Using a cellular phone Bruno would be able to connect with friends in any town in the country. He could send and receive information about local conditions. He might discover that it was raining in the south, snowing in the north, hot and dry in the west and windy in the east. Each of these friends and *each of these locations exists now* outside his present location and Bruno can get information from them while he's sitting on the train (his now point).

Bruno can use the information he receives from the future to make decisions. When he discovers it's cold in the North he might decide to briefly leave the train at the next stop and buy a sweater. Without this information, he'd arrive unprepared.

I believe this story provides a better way to understand the workings of your consciousness than a model which says getting information from the future is impossible and that *day dreaming* is of little value.

This story is a perfect metaphor for what you do every time you plan a dinner party. You mentally connect with the future and use the information you receive to modify your plans. If you think that a friend might bring two guests, you can take more chairs out of storage, just in case.

> *The model we use to understand something determines the information we receive as well as the information we ignore.*

Learning from the past and the future

The model we use to understand something determines the information included as well as the information that is left out. Thinking of the mind as simply a *recorder* of information rather than a *creator* of information limits your ability to learn from the past and the future.

Learning to connect with the possible future is the secret of every successful person and explains why goal-setting is such an important skill. The more precisely you can identify a future goal,

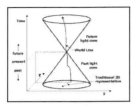

the more accurate and valuable is the information you receive from it.

Viewing your mind through the metaphor of Bruno's train trip gives you a huge advantage. If Einstein was right, *you can gather information from any area of inner spacetime*. This includes a past that didn't happen, a present you are not physically experiencing and a future that may never happen. Using your mind to gather such information gives you an edge over someone who can't, enabling you to live life more effectively. I believe the story of Bruno's train trip explains in simple terms the difference between those who are successful and happy and those who are not.

Learning new lessons from the past

To learn from the past, Bruno simply calls his southern friend and asks, *What happened after I left?* This gives him more information about a past that still exists. The same opportunity is available to you. When you mentally revisit a painful past experience and ask, *What lessons can I learn from this?* You are using the past as a source of increasingly valuable information.

When you ask yourself, *If I had acted differently in this past situation, what different effect might have been created?* you get information about a whole range of virtual realities, each of which can be a source of continued learning and growth. Learning to use your imagination like this means the whole of your past becomes a resource.

Learning from the future

This metaphor also means a spectrum of possible futures can provide valuable information if you will just learn to ask yourself the appropriate questions.

When you ask yourself, *What might I do if A happens or if B happens?* you are immediately plugged into a series of virtual

84

futures and are given an opportunity to plan for various possibilities.

When you ask yourself, *If A happens, what opportunities would be created for me?* you'll be able to take advantage of even an unwanted situation.

If you make a mistake and ask yourself, *How could I change my approach the next time so I fair better?* information floods into your mind from the past allowing you to improve your future performance. In this way a negative event can become positive and something you once called a failure can give you an advantage.

The past doesn't have to remain as it was. You can change it. By asking yourself the right questions you can eliminate failure from your life altogether. If you've been putting something off because you've been afraid to fail, a source of fear is eliminated from both your inner and outer worlds! The implications of this one idea can change your life forever.

> *Each virtual reality making up inner space-time is equally able to deliver information to you in the present.*

The possibility of using all of inner space-time as a resource is contained in the metaphor of Bruno's train trip. Each virtual reality making up inner space-time is equally able to deliver information to you in the present. By viewing the mind as a time machine, able to gather information from *any region* of inner space-time, you get to take advantage of an ability most people are not even aware of.

If the imagination really is a wormhole, it provides a doorway to a whole series of other worlds. The real choice each of us has to make is, *Which universe to I wish to live in?* and the real question we need to ask is, *What information from which reality would be most valuable to me in my present situation?*

For Bruno to take full advantage of the information available to him, he needs three things. He needs to *have* a phone, to know *how* to use it and to know *where* to call in order to get the information he requires.

When you perfect your ability to use questions to gather information using the cosmic telephone you were born with, your life opens up in a way that would be impossible from a Newtonian perspective. The power available to you rivals the power available to the Captain of the *Starship Enterprise*, as he travels to distant parts of the universe, learning lessons he can apply to his own life.

The pipeline of your imagination gives you a huge advantage. It connects you to all the past, all the future and every parallel present. It connects you to new worlds still to be created by *you*, creator of worlds!

As you systematically develop your newly discovered abilities, your advantage will increase. When you recognize the great and marvelous power you were born with, your life will be changed forever.

The following chapters contain explicit instructions on how to use your new-found *cosmic connection* in a number of exciting ways. What would you rather do... chug along as a passenger on a seventeenth century steam train, or whiz along as the captain of your very own star ship?

The choice is yours... and what a choice it is!

Chapter Thirteen

The Key to Your Personal Power

*To walk without pain you can either
cover the world with leather
or cover your feet with leather*

The Buddha

This chapter marks a turning point in the development of your personal power. The preceding chapters have discussed how we each create our personal reality unconsciously. From this point on you will begin consciously influencing this process. This is exciting. It marks the transition from being the victim of circumstances to participating in their creation.

Understanding the connection between your thinking and your world gives you insight into how you can use your mind as a creative force, because changing your internal reality transforms your outer reality automatically. This chapter and the ones that follow contain a variety of tools for making specific internal changes that will attract more of what you want while eliminating what you don't want.

Moving from reacting to creating

You may have heard the little story that goes, For the want of a nail the shoe was lost. For the want of the shoe the horse was lost. For the want of the horse the rider was lost. For the want of the rider the message was lost. For the want of the message the battle was lost. For the want of the battle the kingdom was lost ... all for the want of a horseshoe nail.

At first glance, the story seems to illustrate how a seemingly insignificant detail can have huge consequences. But the point of the story is more subtle than this, because the reason the nail was lost was due to the rider's attitude. Had he been more aware and checked the condition of the nail, the outcome of the battle would have been very different. So the significant aspect of the story was not the nail, but the rider's thoughts about the nail.

You'll soon find that the key which unlocks your personal power is just as subtle.

The point of view with which you have been viewing life is not the truth. It just seems like it to you. Your reality is created as a by-product of the questions you have been asking yourself. When you stop asking, Why are these things happening to me? and begin asking, What concepts and beliefs would create the conditions and circumstances I want? you gain great insight into how you can use your thinking to transform your life. When you begin asking, What do I need to change in myself to create more of what I want? you gain insight into the internal changes that can trigger desired changes in your outer world. Choosing to ask yourself a different set of questions moves you from reacting to creating. The difference in the two words is the position of one letter. But the implications of this tiny change are massive.

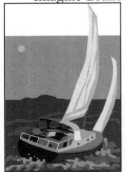

Imagine Bruno sitting in a sailboat in the middle of the ocean. If he doesn't know how the sails and rudder work, he has no power. His boat is pushed about by the wind and the tide. He has no choice but to watch the sails flapping in the breeze, hoping he gets blown toward a safe haven. Ignorance makes him a victim of circumstances.

But as he learns to operate the sails and rudder, he undergoes a transformation. The wind, once his enemy, suddenly becomes his ally. No matter which way it blows a small adjustment keeps him moving in the right direction. He ceases being a victim of external conditions and begins exercising influence over his life. Awareness has made him a person of power.

A similar change takes place in you as you begin to choose the contents of your mind. Because the content with which the mind automatically operates has changed, so has the effect. When you take charge of your internal environment, the external circumstances of your life are transformed. You continue moving in the direction you have chosen. Your life begins to contain progressively more circumstances of the kind you have chosen.

The choice to participate in this awakening is entirely yours. To access and use this power you need to do only one thing: learn to decide for yourself what things mean.

The meaning creates the feeling

At first glance, it appears that our feelings are triggered by external events, but this is not accurate. Our feelings result from the meaning of the event, and the interpretation is our choice. We make unconscious choices about the meaning of each event we experience, but the decisions happen so quickly we're not aware we're doing anything. The process has become modularized. To develop our power it is crucial that we learn to intercede in this process.

Events often happen for no apparent reason. As children we made judgments about the world which continue to spawn unwanted events and uncomfortable feelings. If we find ourselves experiencing repeated patterns of events, we know the ultimate cause is some pattern of thought, but how do we discover which thought pattern is the culprit?

The key to unlocking this cycle is to understand the difference between a triggering cause and a structuring cause.

Triggering and structuring causes

In Newton's model of the universe every event had an absolute, physical cause. In Einstein's model events have both a physical and a non physical cause, and how much of each depends upon the frame of reference. American philosopher Fred Dretske has developed a pair of concepts he calls a structuring cause and a triggering cause, which help us understand this process.

Here's how he explains it: The thermostat in your home is connected to the furnace in such a way that it switches on when the temperature drops and switches off when the temperature rises. Temperature, thermostat and furnace form a feedback loop in which the wiring is the structuring cause and the drop in temperature is the triggering cause.

Neither one by itself is enough to turn on the furnace. Both are necessary. Although the triggering cause for the furnace coming on (the temperature) is totally unpredictable, the structuring cause (the wiring) is set up by you.

If the wiring is correct, everything is fine, but faulty wiring can result in a variety of effects from the same triggering cause. If the thermostat is mistakenly connected to the garage door opener, a drop in temperature will open the garage! If your neighbour's thermostat is connected to the outside lights, a drop in temperature will turn her lights on! Since the triggering cause is the same in both cases, the different effects are due entirely to different *structuring* causes.

This insight into the dual nature of causality gives us a fresh insight into how our emotions work. The triggering cause for our emotions is an external event but the structuring cause is our *interpretation* of what the event means. Something one person finds amusing can make another angry and a third depressed. For people unaware of the role of a structuring cause, emotions seem directly connected to external events. Since events are inherently unpredictable, life becomes a nightmare for these people. They blame external events for how they feel. Their inability to recognize the role of meaning makes them victims of circumstances they are powerless to change. This is the bad news.

The good news is that for each of us, the internal mechanism that actually creates our emotions can be controlled. Each unconscious pattern of meaning and reaction is due to a combination of concepts and beliefs we have created and which we can change, once we figure out what's going on.

Gaining control

We each need to design structuring causes that allow unpredictable events to happen without producing negative effects, leaving us free to enjoy life without worrying about what might happen or what somebody might do. This empowers us to take action toward our goals without being stopped by negative emotions. If you believe the world is unfriendly,  you've set up the structuring cause for a life of struggle and frustration. If you believe there is something wrong with you or that you lack some essential ingredient for success, your life will consist of continual internal stress and external conflict.

You need to develop a belief that the world is friendly, or at least neutral; that events don't mean anything; that you deserve happiness; that the easiest way to succeed is to relax and do what you enjoy doing.

You need to develop a concept of other people as friendly and supportive of your goals. With this mind set, when something doesn't work out as expected, you won't take it personally. You'll treat it as a learning experience. Your disappointment will pass quickly. You'll make a small internal adjustment and get back on course. Developing these beliefs and adopting these concepts is entirely under your control.

As the quote from the Buddha at the beginning of the chapter indicates, you can spend your life trying to avoid painful situations or you can change the mind set which is the real cause of your pain. Taking responsibility for the contents of your mind means finding a point of view that puts you in control of your emotions. It means not reading too much into individual events and focusing instead on creating patterns of events more in alignment with the life you've chosen to enjoy.

Choosing the meaning of events

Your mind is constantly creating concepts, explanations and

expectations as effortlessly as nature creates flowers and trees. As in the example of the footprints on the beach, the mind is constantly creating information by asking questions and answering them. This determines what it focuses on and the meaning it gives to them. Your job is to consciously intercede in this process so your mind creates more parts of the life you've chosen. You do this by controlling the questions you ask yourself.

> *Learning to ask empowering questions while simultaneously feeling positive emotions is one of the most important skills you can develop.*

You repeatedly experience the same patterns of circumstances and the same feelings because you habitually ask yourself the same questions. This determines the focus of both your inner and outer awareness. Learning to ask empowering questions while simultaneously feeling positive emotions is the most important skill you can develop.

If you were to ask yourself each morning, "What positive things do I have to feel thankful for today?" it would soon become a habit. You'd ask yourself the question without thinking. It would eventually move from being a conscious, verbal organizing principle to an unconscious, non-verbal one, directing your mind to notice things to be grateful for. Your perceptions would shift. Your beliefs would shift too, stimulating a steady stream of positive feelings in your body.

As the filtering effect of this attitude would automatically be projected outward, you'd notice a never-ending stream of things in your life to feel grateful for. You'd notice how lucky you were. It would seem to you that your life was full of positive things. Your life would have changed for the better. All because of a new habit of asking a certain kind of question.

Worry is the effect of the non-verbal question, "What negative things might happen in the near future?" It automatically produces negative thought forms and negative expectations. This causes more worry and makes one perceive events in a negative light.

When feeling afraid you are really asking yourself, "What pain might I feel?" This stimulates more painful feelings, causes thought forms of painful possibilities, and traps you in a spiral of ever increasing fear.

A feeling of confidence is really the non verbal question, "How might I successfully deal with an unforeseen event?" This way of looking at the world will stimulate a constant stream of positive thought forms and positive feelings, leading to increasing confidence, personal power and success.

Ask yourself an empowering question

When something happens that triggers a negative feeling, you can break this cycle by asking yourself these questions:

- What exactly am I feeling as I think about this situation?
- What would I have to believe to feel this way?
- How am I conceiving this situation?
- How could I interpret this event to feel good about it?
- What could I believe that would make this process automatic?

These questions will change your mental focus. You'll become more aware of the pattern of concepts, beliefs and expectations that are really causing your negative feelings. You'll become aware of a greater variety of choices available to you.

93

As you learn to monitor your thinking and your feelings on an on-going basis, you'll become like an experienced sailor adjusting his sails to take advantage of changing wind patterns. With experience you'll learn how to make a steady series of minor internal adjustments that will keep your personality on balance and your life on course.

Any situation that seems to be causing you pain indicates you are giving it a meaning that triggers a negative feeling in you, unconsciously giving the world power over how you feel. Asking yourself empowering questions makes you aware of the unconscious patterns that are giving your power away like this. The instant you catch yourself doing this you can change. Like the messenger in the story, your increased awareness allows you to fix the nail that makes the difference between winning and losing in life.

The process of rooting out unconscious negative thought patterns and replacing them with positive ones will change your personality. It will change your reality. Controlling the questions you ask yourself will influence the contents of your mind and the contents of your life. Just as your ability to put on a pair of shoes allows you to walk around without pain, your ability to choose the meaning of any event is the key to enjoying more of your life.

.

Chapter Fourteen
Attitude

Your attitude, not your aptitude,
determines your altitude.

Rev. Jesse Jackson

No one denies the importance of attitude. A poor attitude about work makes your job a drudgery and damages your chances for advancement. A poor attitude about your partner will have immediate and lasting effects on your relationship. A poor attitude about life will create stress in your world, play havoc with your emotions and affect your health. Your attitude determines the impact an unexpected event has on your life. Even the most negative event can be a source of positive growth when viewed in an empowering manner.

But what exactly is an attitude? Is it internal or external? a cause or an effect? the result of something or a determining factor in its outcome? An attitude is all these things, yet it is very easy to explain.

> *An attitude is a frame of reference that gives an event meaning.*

Your attitudes shape and color your thinking, giving it tone and texture. They influence not only *what* you perceive but *how* you perceive it. Your attitude about any event determines its meaning, changing your feelings and your behavior in reaction to it. Since your behavior is the structuring cause for your experience, your attitudes ultimately affect the content of your world.

Changing your attitudes enables you to control your feelings and your reaction to events. This shift from unconscious reacting to conscious creating is the key to setting up the structuring cause for a life of your own design. As your life increasingly takes on the structure you have decided to experience, you move from being a victim of life to being the conscious creator of it.

To get some idea of how your mind creates attitudes and the effects they have, try this little exercise.

Attitude Exercise

Answer this question ... On a scale of ten, how friendly are dogs? Whatever number you get as an answer represents one of your unconscious attitudes about dogs. It might remain unconscious forever. But you immediately become aware of it as soon as you ask the question. But if you think your answer contains any information about dogs you have confused your map for the territory.

Notice the images, sounds and feelings that come to you as you slowly read and think about the following words ...

school ... work ... mother ... father ... money ... sex ... relationships ... success ... failure ... the past ... the future ... happiness ... woman ... man ... love ...

The thoughts and feelings triggered by these words indicate some very specific things about your unique map of the world. As you become aware of your limiting attitudes and change them, you remove their effects from your life. When you add a new, positive attitude to your mind you experience its positive effects.

Psychologists tell us that the main structure of our attitudes is formed by the age of eight, so we see the world through the eyes of an eight-year-old. The stress you feel comes from trying to squeeze your life into the conceptual framework of an eight-year-old. How much do you think your emotions, your personal power and your success are influenced by this effort? If you want to develop power over your circumstances you will have to let go of these outdated thinking patterns and adopt new ones.

Your attitudes are a non-verbal mental language. The development of your attitudes parallels the development of your speech. You learned to speak as a child from copying your parents. You can't remember learning to speak and are unaware of the unconscious movements of nerve and muscle used in speaking. The way you construct sentences, your tone of voice, and the rhythm of your speech all developed before the age of eight. Although your accent identifies you as one of tens of thousands of people from your part of the country, a friend can pick your voice out of a jumble of conversations in a crowded restaurant. Amazing, isn't it?

The unique nature of your voice is mirrored by the unique nature of your attitudes and the unique meaning you give to your life. Although you've experienced virtually the same past as thousands of others, the reality you have created for yourself is as unique as your voice.

The structure creates the meaning

Both your speech and your thinking are made up of smaller units which have no meaning until assembled into patterns. Consider these two sentences ...

- "John hit the ball."
- "The ball hit John."

The words in these two sentences are exactly the same, yet the meanings are quite different, as are the implications. Another agent is implied in the second sentence even though none is mentioned. Both the meaning and the implication of these sentences are due to the *arrangement*. The words *hit*, *ball* and *John* can each mean a number of things.

No event of your life has any meaning until you give it one with your attitude.

97

Your personal reality consists of the meaning your attitude gives to the events of your life. You created this pattern of attitudes before the age of eight.

You can't control the way events unfold but you can control the meaning you give them. To change your life you simply need to adopt a new attitude. Placing things in a different context changes the tone of your life and gives you a new level of personal power.

Attitudes focus and filter the senses

You can't possibly pay attention to all of the data bombarding your senses each minute of the day. Your attitudes filter some things out and other things in, making you blind to some aspects of your experience and acutely aware of others. Lovers are blind to their partners' faults. Buy a new car and it seems everyone is driving one. Adopt a new attitude and you see its effects everywhere.

Attitudes affect memory and expectation

Your attitudes affect both your inner and outer senses, influencing what you perceive in both your outer and inner worlds. Your expectations of *what* the future holds and *how* it will unfold, your memory of *what* happened in the past, what it *means* and *how* it influences your life today are all affected by your attitudes.

> *Changing an attitude changes your past your present and your future.*

Attitudes are both causes and effects

An attitude starts out as a hypothesis, created by your explainer, but once adopted becomes a structuring cause. A person with the attitude *life is fun* will experience more pleasure than someone with the attitude *life is hard*. She'll do things the fun way, get results with less effort and enjoy the game of life. The second person will expect problems and encounter them. She'll feel badly when things don't work out and tend to give up sooner. Each will experience the results their attitudes lead them to expect. Each will focus on aspects of the past and future that agree with their attitude, making them become stronger over time. The Chinese say, *As the twig is bent, so grows the tree.*

People are as blind to their attitudes as to their voice tone, experiencing the same patterns of events repeatedly, unaware they are doing it to themselves. Learning how to modify your attitudes opens the door to a flood of new experiences and new ways of enjoying life. A new attitude leads to new beliefs and more personal power. Your attitudes are the keys to your new world.

The right attitude

Growing up under the often critical eye of parents, we learn that certain things are right and others wrong. Many people still see life this way, but absolute right or wrong is a Newtonian concept. Any attitude that creates stress in yourself or another does no one any good. Rather than asking yourself, *What's the right thing to do?* asking yourself, *What is the appropriate attitude under the circumstances?* helps you discover the point of view leading to the results you want. A positive attitude is one that allows you to accept the reality of the situation, allows you to feel good and supports your learning and growth. To operate out of habit when conditions have changed causes problems. Constantly reevaluate your attitudes in light of your present circumstances.

Is an attitude a thing or a process?

An attitude is the frame of reference giving meaning to an event, but if we forget that thinking is a dynamic activity we will confuse the *arranging* of the pieces for the *arrangement*. This is like confusing the driving with the route driven. To conceive an attitude as a thing is a perfect example of a *nominalization*. This robs us of our power to modify them. An attitude is an automatic, unconscious behavior pattern similar to dancing, speaking or tying your shoelaces. It is a process that can easily be changed.

To illustrate how easily meanings can change, we'll use the same sentence as before, simply altering our tone of voice while saying it. Try it and you'll see what I mean.

Changing Meanings

Say this sentence aloud ...	John hit the ball.
Now say this one ...	John hit the ball?
Now this one ...	<u>John</u> hit the ball?
And this one ...	<u>John</u> ... hit the ball!

Changing your tone of voice alters the process, giving four different meanings to the very same arrangement of words. Is a sentence a thing or a process? Is voice tone a thing, or a process? An attitude is exactly this kind of dynamic activity.

Your attitude about life is just a habit

You've been tying your shoelaces the same way for decades but can change this pattern today if you want to. With a little awareness you can change an ineffective attitude just as easily. If you conceive memories as things and believe feelings are caused by events you endow our past with extraordinary power over you and imply you are powerless to change your situation because past events can't be changed. This attitude makes you a victim ... not a victim of your past but a victim of your point of view.

The past has no meaning. It's only a thought form. Your attitude about it is no more fixed than your voice tone or the way you tie your shoelaces. Changing your attitude about the past creates a ripple effect that spreads outward, touching every aspect of your life. The focus of your thinking shifts. Your mind puts together the data of your senses in new ways. You notice new things. Your life takes on new meaning. Negative events become transformed into sources of power. By exercising this power to change an attitude we regain stewardship over the course of our lives. We erase negative emotions and discover resources to which we have remained blind because of our limited view of ourselves.

In the next chapter I will share with you the most powerful technique I have ever learned for uncovering limiting attitudes and changing them.

Chapter Fifteen

The Affirmation Principle

It is the mind that maketh good of ill, that maketh
wretch or happy, rich or poor.

Edmund Spenser

The Affirmation Principle is the most effective way of gaining insight into your attitudes and easiest way of changing them.

You can use the Affirmation Principle to do three specific things:

To discover your negative attitudes.

To erase negative attitudes from your mind.

To insert positive attitudes into your mind.

Don't confuse this technique with other uses of affirmations you may have learned elsewhere. This is a specific tool for a specific purpose.

Here's how it works.

Take a sheet of paper and divide the page like this.

Affirmation   Response

_____ _____

_____ _____

_____ _____

In the last chapter I wrote that no event means anything ***unless*** and ***until*** it is placed within a specific frame of reference which gives it a meaning.

The purpose of the Affirmation Principle is to make you aware of the structure of these frames of reference so you can modify them.

Events with similar meanings are linked together in your mind, forming **networks of references** supporting specific attitudes. For example, if I ask you, 'On a scale of ten, how friendly are dogs?' you might answer '8' meaning you think dogs are friendly, or '2', meaning you think they are not very friendly. A person who answers '2' might even be afraid of them.

Every attitude you have is supported by specific **references** (examples) the way a table is supported by legs.

So, no matter what your attitude about dogs -- no matter what number you get in response to the question -- you'll be able to bring to mind a number of **examples** of times when dogs were friendly (or unfriendly) to support your point of view.

A person with an '8' attitude will have lots of '8' (positive) references. A person with a '2' attitude will have lots of '2' (negative) references.

If you want to strengthen any attitude, you simply need to add more references (supports) to it. If you want to weaken it, you remove the supports. When all supports are removed the attitude will disappear.

Step 1: Uncovering specific negative attitudes

We can use the 'affirmation principle' to uncover specific negative attitudes and the references that support these attitudes.

For the purpose of this exercise, an affirmation is considered to be any **general, positive** statement which represents a possible way of looking at things. It might be quite different than the way you are looking at things now.

Step One: - Write the affirmation on the left side of the page and read it over a few times. Get yourself into the **state of mind**

where you *feel* the affirmation is true. *Imagine* looking at your past, your present and your future through the eyes of a person to whom the affirmation *really is true*.

Step Two: - Pay attention to the specific, negative responses that your mind gives you in response to the affirmation. Write these in the 'response' column.

Suppose we begin with the affirmation, 'I succeed at everything I try.'

Because you don't really have this attitude yet, your mind will *react* by presenting you with specific negative responses, saying in effect, 'This affirmation is not true and here's why.' Write these responses on the right side of the page.

These responses are very important. They identify the references which are supporting the *opposite attitude* to the positive one represented by the affirmation.

These events have acquired a *negative meaning* and have become lodged in your subconscious mind where they are *working against you below the surface*, creating situations and circumstances you don't want.

When Joel Kapusta, who attended one of my seminars in Vancouver, tried this exercise, here's what he reported to the rest of the room ...

'When I started using the affirmation, 'I succeed at everything I attempt.' My first response was a big, 'No way!' I felt it was a joke. As I wrote the affirmation again, I got another specific response, 'I even failed math in grade six.'

Joel continued, 'When I thought about it, I realized that this event had been lurking in my mind for years, supporting the negative attitude, 'Learning is a pain.' which has been a belief of mine and a negative part of my self-image since grade six.'

Using the *Affirmation Principle* with this affirmation made Joel aware of a specific negative attitude about life and about himself that had been causing him inner conflict for years.

As he explained it, during his school years, every time he had to study something, he felt immediately negative about it, anticipating problems.

This negative meaning had unconsciously been created by Joel's 'explainer' when he was twelve years old.

Once he became aware of this negative attitude, he was ready for the next step, erasing the negative attitude from his mind.

Step 2: Erasing specific negative attitudes

I led him to examine how this past event had acquired this negative meaning and to explore if we could give it another interpretation.

We discovered that he had changed schools near the end of grade six, an event which had influenced his performance on the math test. Because he joined the class late in the year, he was not up to speed with the rest of the class and failed the final.

As we explored his history we found that he was good at learning lots of things. He was an accomplished skier and scuba diver, could play guitar and speak Polish and German.

Together we reframed the memory of the math exam in grade six to mean, 'External circumstances can influence my performance'.

When asked what his achievements in sports, music and languages could mean, he came up with the statement, 'I'm good at learning things I enjoy.'

This is an entirely different attitude than, 'Learning is a pain.' and the expression on his face as he stood in front of the room showed it.

For Joel, this simple exercise highlighted a *specific event* which had acquired a *negative* meaning, and which had unconsciously influenced his life for years. A simple analysis of the event revealed that the negative meaning had no real foundation and had blinded him to abilities he'd been taking for granted.

With this negative attitude gone, his self esteem experienced an immediate increase.

All Joel needs to do to is to strengthen this new attitude toward learning by spending a few minutes each day reviewing his past through the 'lens' of this new attitude. As new, positive memories come to him, he needs to write down the references.

The more references he can think of, the stronger the new attitude will become.

With a new attitude about learning, Joel will be more open to learning new things. He will anticipate more success. Linking learning to *enjoyment* rather than *pain* will affect other areas of his life too. It will lower his level of stress and open doors to new opportunities.

To erase a negative attitude, all you need to do is take each of your negative responses and ask yourself,

What does this event mean?

Why does it mean this?

Could it mean something positive?

Make a list of possible ways of viewing this event until you find a way that shifts its negative meaning to one that's at least neutral, and perhaps even positive.

As the *meaning* shifts, this event will no longer support the negative attitude, and it will become weaker.

Once all its supports are removed, the negative attitude will simply disappear from you mind to be replaced by *the positive affirmation* you were using that triggered the negative response.

Its negative effects will disappear from your life, to be replaced by the positive effects of the positive attitude.

Your perception of the past, the present and the future will shift. You'll feel better about your life and your future will unfold differently.

Step 3: Inserting a positive attitude into your mind

Depending on the affirmation used, you may find that it triggers a whole host of negative responses, revealing a great number of negative attitudes.

It doesn't matter. Simply continue the process.

As you systematically *eliminate the references* for the attitude that is opposing the positive affirmation, your mind will begin to *accept the new affirmation* as a valid statement about your reality.

As you continue to consciously view life through the filter of this new attitude you will begin to notice more and more events from the past and present that confirm it.

If you make a list of these positive, supportive references and begin living your life through the filter of this new point of view, it will eventually sink down into your subconscious mind where it will begin automatically working for you under the surface.

It will begin *filtering in* sense data that conforms to it and *filtering out* sense data which doesn't.

You will begin to *expect* more positive situations *in the future* that resonate with it.

You will automatically find more supportive references. Over time your new attitude will take root and grow in strength. Your perception of reality will shift. Over time the new, positive affirmation may eventually become one of your more predominant attitudes.

The Importance of Mental Gardening

By choosing your affirmations, you can probe a specific part of your mind, uncovering specific negative events and attitudes which have been unconsciously working against you in this area of your life.

As you continue to work with the *Affirmation Principle*, you will become aware of progressively larger areas of your inner reality.

Working with your attitudes is *mental gardening*.

This is a very important practice in which you simultaneously *root out the old* as you *cultivate the new*.

It's not unusual to encounter negative attitudes with roots stretching back to early childhood, with a large number of supportive references.

These attitudes will seem *so true* you may have a hard time even imagining another way of looking at life.

But such an attitude is simply a large mental structure with many legs. When you remove its references it will wither like a tree whose roots have been cut. Numerous areas of your life it has been interfering with will become transformed.

You can count on it.

Sample affirmations

Any general, positive statement will help you uncover specific negative attitudes which are inhibiting the natural flow of your creative energy. With practice, you'll be able to create affirmations that apply to your specific situation. In the meantime, here are some sample affirmations you can experiment with. These represent attitudes you might want to plant in your mind. Any specific negative references these affirmations trigger should be examined carefully, their meanings changed.

Affirmations about your goals ...

"I deserve all I desire"

"All my goals are attainable"

"The more fun I have, the more successful I become"

"I easily achieve all my goals"

"My written plan is the road map to the future I desire"

"Nothing is holding me back"

Affirmations about love ...

"I feel love all around me"

"I am loved and I love freely"

"All my relationships are perfect"

"I am always appreciated"

" I love myself "

"The more I love, the more I am loved"

"I deserve to be loved"

"I attract ideal lovers easily"

Affirmations about money ...

"Money is good"

"I deserve to have lots of money"

"All my investments are profitable"

"I save money easily"

"My net worth is increasing steadily"

"I like money and money likes me"

"Money is my friend"

Affirmations about sex

"Sex is fulfilling"

"I enjoy sex"

"Sex is the highest form of communication"

"Good sex is good medicine"

"Women appreciate me and I appreciate them"

"Men appreciate me and I appreciate them"

"Sex is a spiritual communion with another"

"In sex, I give and receive equally"

"The more I trust sex, the more it rewards me"

Affirmations about health . . .

"My body is perfectly healthy"
"I have a beautiful body, and I respect it"
"I love my body"
"My body loves me"
"My body is my friend"
"I get plenty of exercise"
"I am full of energy"
" I have lots of enthusiasm "
"My weight is perfect"
"I have a naturally beautiful body"

Affirmations about spirituality

"God is on my side"
"I live in a safe universe"
"The universe supplies all my needs and desires"
"I am naturally spiritual"
"I love myself and the universe in which I live now"
"The power of the universe works for me"
"The laws of the universe are for my advantage"
"The powers of the universe flow through me"
"The universe is my playground"
"I deserve all the good of the universe"

Affirmations about relationships ...

"My relationships are perfect"
"Those I love, love me"
"The more love I accept, the more I receive"
"I trust others and others trust me"

"I enjoy an ever expanding circle of friends"

"I attract ideal lovers naturally and easily"

"I am naturally attractive"

"I have all the friends I want"

"My relationships are always fulfilling"

Affirmations about success ...

"All my limitations are imaginary"

"I have unlimited opportunities"

"Everything works out to my advantage"

"I deserve all the good I desire"

"I can't fail"

"I enjoy making mistakes, because I learn from them"

"I am getting more successful every day"

"Obstacles provide their own solutions"

"I am easily successful"

"I am a winner, with a long history of success"

Strengthen your new attitudes

Your new attitudes need to be nourished regularly if they are to grow. Do this by sitting quietly and imagining yourself going through your day as though this new point of view were already an established part of your life. Use your imagination as a creative force.

Spend a few minutes each day contemplating the implications of your new attitude. Imagine performing future tasks as a person with this attitude. You'll soon find yourself viewing ever larger areas of your life through the filter of this attitude.

Combine the use of the Affirmation Principle with this visualization exercise in a quiet, relaxed mood when you have the opportunity to feel the effect. The idea is to coax your mind into giving up a few of its secrets. Be gentle with yourself. Expect positive results. Adopt the attitude that you deserve to become the person you desire to be, that mental gardening represents a natural stage of your personal growth. Adopt the attitude that developing your personal power is good for you and good for others. Cultivate a win/win attitude.

Establish a daily routine.

Work with the Affirmation Principle for a few minutes each day. Before long you'll gain a great deal of valuable insight. Your perception of yourself and of your world will shift. You'll gain the power to influence your mind and your circumstances.

Chapter Sixteen

Beliefs, Emotions and States

> *You have the resources to solve any*
> *problem or achieve any goal.*
> *You need only access them effectively.*
>
> Anthony Hamilton

Your thoughts are arranged in a hierarchy in which the thinking at each level is more subtle than the level below it and exerts control over it. Three levels of this pyramid are *attitudes, beliefs* and *states.* We've already covered the role attitudes play in influencing the way your mind's automatic mental processes create your life. Let's move on now to the role played by beliefs and states.

Beliefs

All your life you've been trying to figure out how the world works and the results of your efforts are your beliefs about how it operates. You think your beliefs represent truths about the world but this is an illusion. They are merely another level of your mind's unconscious organizing principles.

Here is a general definition we will use for discussion purposes:

A belief is a feeling of certainty about the meaning of something

Attitudes are mental processes which create meaning. Beliefs are these same mental processes connected to your body, creating patterns of feeling which add color, texture and tone to your thinking. Depending upon the intensity of the feeling, these can be further subdivided into *opinions, beliefs* and *convictions*. If you have several opinions on a subject and are not sure what it all means, you'll make a decision based on what *feels* right. This is your belief on the subject. You think it's the truth, but only your truth. Controlling your beliefs means controlling both your attitude and your feelings.

 Most peoples' feelings occur in reaction to events, making them victims of external conditions. By controlling your reactions you gain the ability to act unencumbered by negative feelings, setting up structuring causes for more of what you want. In the example about the friendliness of dogs, ten people who each have a different number on this internal scale will each have specific examples of encounters with dogs they take to be definitive ... references they unconsciously use to support their belief. Simply thinking about dogs will make people at the low end of the scale feel badly and people at the high end feel good. If a person with a low number could learn to feel comfortable while thinking of dogs, her attitude would change and her world would suddenly contain friendlier dogs. This would allow her to function differently around dogs and enjoy a greater variety of experiences.

Your beliefs affect your emotions and your logic

A belief links your left and right brains, your feelings and your logic, forming a feedback loop affecting both your *perceptions* of reality and your *explanations* about it. Events trigger feelings related to your belief about what it means and you decide on the meaning of the event by what feels right. A different belief leads to a different feeling and a different explanation of reality and a strong conviction distorts both your perception and your reasoning, leading to explanations which make you feel better, but which may be far from accurate.

114

Your beliefs are the laws of your world

Beliefs determine how you interpret events. Things mean what you believe they do. Your reality is what you believe it is. Your beliefs determine your expectations. When things don't unfold as expected you'll experience a range of emotions, ranging from mild curiosity because things don't quite fit, to absolute terror that your world is falling apart. Beliefs determine your behavior. You won't do things you believe will lead to a negative feeling.

Your beliefs form the boundaries of your world

Your beliefs determine what exists in your world, forming the boundary between the real and the unreal. If you believe in angels you will see evidence for them. If you believe in obstacles you will encounter them. If you believe obstacles are simply *conditions*, you will never encounter obstacles, only more or less acceptable conditions.

By defining your terms creatively you can remove from your world all resistance to the life you want to create.

Your beliefs are not true

They are just the operating principles of your model of reality. You believe your perceptions give you factual evidence and that a logical chain of reasoning leads from these facts to what you hold to be truths of the world, but this is an illusion. By unconsciously selecting a point of view that *feels* comfortable, you set your attitudes up to filter in evidence that supports your position and filter out contrary evidence. Since what you take as the truth comes down to what *feels* right, what you accept as evidence is very inner. Over time your beliefs become as integrated into your world view as your tone of

115

voice and since your reality seems consistent, you think you have found the truth, but your evidence is only true in your model of the world.

> *There is no 'truth' only your truth. There is no 'external world' only your external world.*

You can choose what you believe

Your unconscious assumption that your beliefs reflect reality is false because your belief in the existence of reality itself is false. There is no *reality*. There is only *your model of reality*. Belief in a physical reality which can be known is an artifact of the Newtonian model. Each of us is trapped inside our own private frame of reference, dreaming our own private dream. Change your beliefs about reality and you change the only reality available to you.

Your task is not to discover the truth about the world but to cultivate a system of beliefs which creates harmony in your world and frees your creative spirit - to clear out the tangled underbrush in your mind that's causing your unwanted emotions - to replace your out-dated thought hierarchy with a system of concepts, attitudes and beliefs that allows for the creation of a harmonious physical and emotional world, allowing yourself the freedom to create the results you want.

> *Continuous practice with the Affirmation Principle will allow you to do this.*

Emotions

As you go higher in the hierarchy of thought, the intensity of the feeling connected to your point of view increases. To *believe* something means to feel certain your attitude is right. To have a *conviction* about something is to feel your belief is the *truth*. Intense emotions come from making strong judgments about the nature of

116

reality. Fear is a conviction. So is faith.

Having a conviction about something anchors your beliefs into your body in a very intense way.

To feel embarrassed or angry or ashamed means your belief about the situation is firmly set. You won't get highly emotional if someone contradicts an opinion. You will if they attack one of your convictions.

Gaining a personal sense of your power

Experimenting with the Affirmation Principle will inevitably bring your emotions into play. By having the courage to continue searching for other interpretations of experience in spite of your negative feelings you will eventually find one that changes the meaning.

The connection between inner reality and outer reality is determined by you.

At this point you will have made a great discovery - that the connection between inner reality and outer reality is determined by you - that what exists in your world and the position things occupy is a matter of your definition.

Cultivating positive beliefs

As you continue investigating your reality you will find which specific beliefs stimulate which specific emotions and realize that cultivating your belief system is one of the most valuable things you can do, that controlling your beliefs and emotions goes hand in hand with gaining control over both your worlds.

Make lists of your positive and negative emotions and the specific beliefs that trigger them. Eliminating any belief causes the resulting emotion to disappear. Cultivating a belief that causes a positive emotion and you will feel the emotion more. This practice changes your personality and your world.

Clearing out your negative emotions in this way requires skill, courage and persistence. Your first attempts will be confusing but the results will be more than worth the effort. Over time you will gain control over your reactions to unexpected events and your ability to act consistently to create circumstances of your choosing. As you reach deeper into the depths of your unconscious, your emotional pattern will change and your world will begin to conform to the new pattern of belief and expectation you have created.

States

A state is a highly charged mental-physical-emotional-intellectual pattern at the top of the hierarchy of thought. Your states control your beliefs, your emotions and your attitudes. They influence your perceptions, your reasoning and your reactions. Your states define the  ultimate focus of your mind and the ultimate makeup of your reality. They are your convictions made physical.

Your states define your reality. A person in love experiences the world as a wonderful place where everyone is her friend. A person dominated by fear perceives threats on all sides. Her distorted logic supports her feelings and her beliefs, trapping her inside a fearful world. Changing your state changes your reality and the change can be instantaneous. A shift in the tone of someone's voice or the mention of a person's name can send you into a different world. To gain control over your reality you must control your states.

Sorting and controlling your states

Your state at any point in time is the ultimate focusing mechanism of your mind and brain and the identifying mark of the world in which you live. There are hundreds of possible states, but your life is dominated by a dozen or so which you experience on a regular basis.

Your habitual states define your world, your personality, your circle of friends, and your circumstances. The ultimate secret to your success in life will come down to your ability to control your states. Winners are invariably able to control their states and rally their resources to handle situations that would destroy another.

When Sylvester Stallone was trying to finance a script he had written called *Rocky,* he was rejected by over one thousand so-called experts who said it would be impossible to succeed. What would you call the state he had to create to enable himself to carry on?

Total self-confidence?

Tenacity?

Unshakable belief?

Faith?

Absolute commitment?

How much influence did this skill have on his ability to achieve his subsequent success?

Could you develop such a state? How would you do it?

Eliminating negative states

Begin by making a list of negative events and the emotions triggered by them. Choose any emotion as a starting point and ask yourself these questions:

• What would I have to believe to feel this way?

- What am I afraid of?
- What am I expecting?
- How am I conceiving this situation?
- What does this situation mean?

You will soon discover the specific combination of concepts and beliefs necessary to create the negative emotion. To change a concept ask,

How could I conceive this situation in an empowering way?

Insert the new concept into your mind and experience the results. To eliminate a negative belief, use the Affirmation Principle to turn it into its opposite. To opposing beliefs operating on the same situation will cancel each other out.

When the underlying network of concepts and beliefs has been changed you'll no longer feel the emotion in this situation. Repeat this exercise with other situations that trigger the same emotion. In time, no situation will trigger this emotion. When you no longer feel this emotion, the state will also disappear from your world.

Creating positive states

To create a desired state you simply need to control your posture, your breathing and the focus of your mind by asking yourself a set of specific questions. If you practice the following technique five minutes a day for ten days you will soon be able to create any state and maintain it regardless of circumstances. Here's how to use this technique to increase your confidence:

Sit up straight in your chair and ask yourself these questions:

- How do I sit when I feel totally confident?
- How do I breathe when I feel totally confident?

120

- How do I hold the muscles in my face, my forehead, my shoulders, my back and my chest when I feel totally confident?
- What do I say to myself when I feel totally confident?
- What ideas flow through my mind when I feel totally confident?
- How do I imagine the world when I feel totally confident?

You'll notice an immediate shift in your *awareness* and your *feelings* as you do this.

Move your body to change your posture and your breathing as you internally respond to the questions.

Make note of your *posture* and the *ideas* that come to you so the next time you want to feel confident, you'll know how to create this state.

Each time you repeat the exercise, you will become more familiar with the way confidence feels in your body.

Over time, you will be able to create it instantly simply by *holding your body* this way, *breathing* this way and *thinking* this way.

By maintaining a confident state, you empower yourself to handle a difficult situation in the most appropriate manner.

Your confidence changes your present, your past and your future.

Because both memories and expectations are affected by your state, you will be more able to recall times in the past when you were confident and will anticipate the future with more confidence. Your life will take on a different texture and tone. People will see you as a confident person and will begin to act differently toward you. New opportunities will come to you. Your personality and your life will have changed.

121

Practicing this technique with a variety of emotions and states will enable you to create any state instantly. Make a list of positive and empowering states you would like to develop and use this technique to create them for yourself.

The results will be more than worth the effort.

Eliminating negative experiences

Until now your life has largely been one of reacting to the situations in which you have found yourself. Because your beliefs have been unconscious, you've been unaware of the subtle interplay between your mental processes and your reality, concluding that you experience positive and negative emotions because positive and negative things happen to you.

This is false.

A person who conceives reality to operate this way can only escape negative feelings by avoiding negative situations.

Their personal power will keep shrinking and they'll end up avoiding more and more of life until their world is reduced to a small circle of friends and a small number of situations in which they feel comfortable. Either that, or they'll retreat into a fantasy world of alcohol or drugs.

This no-win situation is based upon a misconception. The way out of this cycle of diminishing power is to adopt a new perspective on reality and a more empowering view of your role in it.

Here it is:

Nothing is positive or negative but for the way you interpret it.

Things affect you negatively because your conceptual framework and beliefs trigger this reaction in you. With a different mind set your reaction would be different.

The bad news is that the entire system of concepts, internal maps, beliefs, perception, meaning and emotional reaction is unconscious.

122

The good news is that as you become aware of it you can change it. This is not difficult. You know how to do it already. It just takes time cultivating the contents of your inner world.

As in learning any new discipline, your ability to eliminate negative states and create positive ones will take practice. Think of learning this skill like learning to play a musical instrument.

Give yourself time to perfect your ability.

Be thrilled with your victories.

Over time this skill will prove to be one of your most valued assets in creating the life of your choice.

Chapter Seventeen

Changing the Past

That which doesn't kill me
makes me stronger.

Nietzsche

A Newtonian model nominalizes the present as a thing, masking the true nature of the world as a process. Placing the cause of the present in the past robs us of our power. It makes us victims of something over which we have no control.

In our new model the past is a thought form we create in the present and its effect is due to the meaning we give it. The example of the sentence, "John hit the ball." illustrates that meaning is not created by the concept's <u>parts</u>, but by its <u>tone</u>.

> *The effect of the past is not due to what happened but to the way*
> *we represent it to ourselves.*

This view places power under our control in the present moment, since we can change the effect of the past by changing our concept of it.

Seduced by Newton's model, we have nominalized the entire process. We think of events as physical things with permanent effects and ignore the mind's role in the creation of our world. Like Bruno complaining about his lunch, we complain about the past as though we have nothing to do with it, when it is really a thought form we constantly re-create! The past is like a song we sing over and over again.

When we learn to transform our past by giving it a new meaning, we generate new feelings, new understandings and open up a host of new possibilities.

> *The power to transform your past is available to you right now.*
> *You merely have to remember it in a new way.*

After all, doesn't "re-member" mean "to put together again"? The Chinese say, "You can't put your hand in the river twice." This is because both the river and your hand are different each time. In the same vein we might say, "You can't remember the past twice." Shifting our beliefs to take advantage of this new point of view opens up a world of possibility and power we never knew existed.

Your most valuable tool for doing this is the Affirmation Principle. By using it to analyze how specific past references support specific parts of your present world view, you will uncover the limiting attitudes that are the structuring causes for your present. As you change these you free yourself from a prison you unconsciously created as a child. You also break the cycle of recurring negative emotions in which you have been stuck since then. Like a song writer struggling to compose a new melody, you may have to re-work your new melody many times to find an arrangement that works. Believe me, the payoff is more than worth the effort.

A memory is not something recorded somewhere in your brain. It is an activity similar to playing the piano. Past events do not affect us. The emotions we feel are due to the way we are playing the melody. As we change the process we generate a new set of emotions. We also wake up from the fantasy world in which we have been asleep for years.

Healing your wounds

In a perfect world, we would all enjoy perfect emotional and physical health. We would all have high self-esteem, would be in touch with our talents and be able to reach our goals as easily as we walk to the store to buy a loaf of bread.

But a perfect world is a thought form. And we live in a physical world that bears only a superficial resemblance to the ideal one we imagine.

125

Just as we suffer physical hurts that leave physical scars, disappointments and failed expectations leave scars on our souls. We each enter adulthood with mental and emotional wounds that restrict and limit us.

We have fears. We worry. We have difficulty communicating. We lack self-esteem. We doubt ourselves. We have conflicts in our inner and outer worlds.

Each of us has to learn to live with minor limitations. But if our wounds are so great that they stop us from acting effectively, make us afraid to try something new, or keep us from going for what we want, we need to take some steps to do something about it!

If we can't relax and enjoy ourselves regularly. If we drink too much, smoke too much, eat too much or engage in other unhealthy habits, we need to realize that these behaviors are wound-driven.

Our emotional wounds need to be healed if we are to make any progress toward living a fulfilling life.

How do we do this?

First, we need to *identify* our emotional wounds.

Second, we need to embark on a program to *systematically* heal them. The key word here is 'systematically'. We need to have a system… a program, to heal ourselves step by step.

> ***Healing your emotional wounds is an***
> ***on-going process.***

Identifying our personal wounds and doing the work necessary to heal them requires courage. We need to explore and identify our painful feelings. When we have done this, we need to then take apart the faulty references, distorted interpretations and false beliefs that are the real cause of these painful emotions.

Once we do this, we can restructure our consciousness and allow these wounds to heal. I say allow, because they will heal all by themselves when given the chance.

Doing this liberates our energy, frees our creativity and creates the possibility of experiencing the positive feelings we have been trying ineffectively to experience all along. Coming to terms with the past raises our self-esteem, increases our personal power, improves our health, our emotional balance and the quality of our life.

Depending upon your particular situation, the process may be a long one. A lot of pain will be connected to some of these references and you will feel vulnerable probing for them. My advice at this point would be to seek out a support group or some professional counseling if it seems appropriate.

Be gentle on yourself.

Go at your own pace.

Adopt the attitude that you are doing this because you want to live a healthier emotional and physical life.

Healing these wounds is vitally important if you are to experience the joy you deserve.

Transforming your wounds into blessings

Our new model of consciousness implies the ability to send your inner awareness back in time to the original painful events, then to re-experience them in a new way... to evaluate them in a new light... to give them new meanings…. to create different emotions.

When you do this you transform past painful experiences into powerful learning experiences.

I once heard the poet Robert Bly say that the French word for *wound* is *blessé*, the origin of the English word *blessing*. He explained that the same event causing the wound could also convey a blessing if viewed differently.

Nietzsche said, 'That which doesn't kill me makes me stronger.'

Buddha put it this way, 'Those who hurt you are your best friends, because they point out where you are making your mistakes.'

To transform a painful past event try the following exercise. Choose any negative event and ask yourself these questions:

What am I *telling myself* about this event?

What *conclusions* have I made about it?

How is the way am I *conceiving* this event causing me pain?

How *could I conceive it* so it empowers me?

What *belief* would transform this into a positive experience?

How can I *apply this lesson* to avoid being hurt by this in the future?

As you ask these questions, allow your mind to give you a series of answers, until you find one that makes a difference.

These questions will transform the most damaging events of your life into some of the most empowering,. As you do this you liberate the energy that you have been using to hold these painful experiences in place.

This energy can then be used in healing not only your own life but also the lives of others that you care about.

Developing compassion

I earlier compared physical wounds to emotional ones. If your original pain were caused by a tree branch falling on your head you wouldn't take it personally. You might have a physical scar but no emotional one.

Our emotional scars were created by childhood events involving other people ... people we trusted ... upon whom we counted for protection. When their actions hurt us the emotional scars run deep. But when we examine these people and these events, we discover that our pain implies something that's false and that we have forgotten something that's true.

Our pain implies that these people acted consciously. People are often as unconscious and unaware of the effects of their actions

128

as the tree that drops its branch on your head. There is little point in blaming them. We are just as ignorant on occasion. So the implication that they acted with conscious awareness is false.

We have also forgotten that occasionally our unconscious actions have hurt people. They may blame us even though we had no intention to cause pain. Remembering all this will help us forgive those who's actions have hurt us. Letting go of the <u>meaning</u> of these events releases the <u>pain</u> associated to them.

> ### *A new attitude changes the past and the future simultaneously.*

However I want you to clearly understand something here. I am not suggesting you do this because it's the right thing to do or that you do it for some moral reason. My motives are purely practical. Do it because it stops your pain. Remember a past event with the attitude that someone did it to hurt you, and it hurts. Recall the event with the attitude that your own unconscious interpretation hurt you, and you learn something.

This new attitude changes the past and the future simultaneously. It protects your from pain and allows you to enjoy yourself at the same time.

When we understand our emotional needs and change our interpretations we see that the people we have been blaming were really giving us blessings, since this new knowledge allows us to protect ourselves in the future. Although it may have taken us decades to recognize these blessings, we can still use our increased awareness to improve the quality of our lives in the present and in the future.

The past is not finished. It is evolving. You control its evolution.

The same is true for any concept, including the ones we call mother and father. Changing the way we frame our memories of them gives our relationship with them new meaning. All people were hurt as children either emotionally, verbally, physically, or sexually. Perhaps the feelings associated to these memories have been causing you problems all your life. But it's not too late. You can ease or entirely erase your pain today.

An very wise man once told me a story that changed my perspective on my parents forever, helping to heal many of my own emotional wounds. He said that if a madman were to hit you with a stick, you'd be a fool to get angry with the stick even though it caused you the pain. The stick is merely a passive instrument.

But, he continued, the same is true for the madman. He is as powerless as the stick. He is being driven to act by ignorance and uncontrolled emotions. If you wish to direct your anger at anything it should be directed at ignorance and uncontrolled emotions. These are the true cause of your pain. Parents are simply people, he said. They are largely unaware of their actions. They are slaves to their emotions. In the grip of an uncontrolled emotion they can cause as much pain as a stick wielded by a madman.

As I reviewed my own past in the light of this attitude, the emotions I had associated to past events involving my parents and other people began to heal. This allowed me to recall more positive events I had forgotten. The net effect of this strategy was to alter forever my view of my parents and of my past. It eased my pain and increased my pleasure. I recommend you try this to erase any pain associated to past events.

Increasing your awareness eases your own pain and helps you avoid causing pain to others. When you heal yourself you help all those who come after you.

Develop an attitude of gratitude

The logical extension of this line of reasoning is to reframe all past events and all memories of people which stimulate any pain so they become sources of pleasure. It is not difficult to do. It just takes time. Can you think of a better way to spend fifteen minutes a day than engaged in such an emotional healing period?

As you engage in the process of transforming your past and healing your emotional wounds in this way, you will naturally become more aware of the good things that have happened to you and of the good people you have met. Developing an attitude of gratitude for all the good you have received changes the focus of your mind. An attitude of gratitude creates the structuring cause for more good experiences in the future.

Two thousand years ago, someone asked Jesus Christ how to pray more effectively so he could receive more of the good God had to offer. He replied, "When you pray, give thanks."

It is still the best advice.

Chapter Eighteen

Cultivating the Future

*What you can conceive and
believe you can achieve.*

Napoleon Hill

When I first read ***Think and Grow Rich***, by Napoleon Hill, the above quotation inspired me to embark upon my own personal journey. I wanted to harness this creative inner power, so I began working with my goals and beliefs. I imagined living the life of my choice. But as I did this, I quickly realized something I didn't expect. The above quotation implies we can create our desires by conceiving and believing ***consciously***. But it also describes the ***unconscious*** process of creating what we don't want.

In other words, while I can ***consciously*** create what I consciously conceive and believe, I am already ***unconsciously*** creating what I unconsciously conceive and unconsciously believe. I just have not been aware of it.

The physical world appears out of the future and disappears into the past like an ocean wave traveling past the port hole of a ship. The port hole represents our limited view of the present.

A time-lapse film of the birth, growth and death of an oak tree would show it rise out of the soil, exist for a time, then disappear back into the soil just as a wave disappears into the ocean.

From the perspective of modern physics, a particle does the same. It appears out of a cloud of ***virtual particles***, exists for a time, then disappears back into the quantum field. From a personal perspective, our physical reality materializes out of the non-physical ***possible future*** and disappears into the non-physical past. Both our expectations of the future and our memories of the past are merely shadows of the physical world.

The garden of your mind

One way to visualize the process of creating your reality is to imagine the future as a garden into which you sow the seeds of the present. The seeds of the present are your conscious or unconscious attitudes, beliefs and expectations of what will happen.

Just as flowers appear in response to whatever seeds are planted, your thoughts and expectations create self-fulfilling prophesies which blossom into your physical circumstances.

Expect problems and you will encounter them. Expect to be loved and your world will contain loving people.

But there's more to gardening than simply planting the seeds and waiting for them to mature. If you don't simultaneously remove the young shoots of unwanted plants, they will become full grown weeds choking the life out of the garden you're trying to cultivate.

It's the same in your life. You can create whatever circumstance you wish by cultivating the correct thinking. But if you don't simultaneously eliminate your negative attitudes, beliefs, states and expectations, you'll continue to experience their effect as unwanted circumstances.

Like Job in the biblical story, you'll find yourself saying, 'The things I feared have come upon me.'. To paraphrase Napoleon Hill, what you unconsciously conceive and unconsciously believe you will unconsciously create.

To gain stewardship over your life it's not enough to believe you can create what you want. If you don't eliminate your negative thinking, your life will continue to contain unwanted circumstances as a natural result of the flip side of the same creative process.

In the previous chapter I explained that changing the past will automatically change the future, since the concepts that exist in your future are simply transplanted from the past. Realize that whatever your concept of the future contains will eventually be experienced as some aspect of your physical present. To fully seize your creative power you need to actively cultivate the future by doing two specific things:

- Cultivate the thoughts that produce what you want.
- Stop thinking of what you don't want.

This inner cultivation process means creating a model of the future containing only what you want your life to contain, since *every thought of what you don't want tends to bring it about*. This requires clarity of mind, vigilance and courage. Uncovering these deeply ingrained thought patterns is neither simple nor straightforward.

In chapter eleven I discussed some implications of our new model of the mind. I want to expand upon these implications here and point out some things you need to be aware of if you are serious about creating the life you want.

The reality of the future

Don't be concerned about creating the future. It already exists. You've been creating it all your life, but unconsciously. You've been seeding it with concepts, implications and expectations which continually manifest as your present reality. The longer you remain blind to this, the longer you delay having control over your circumstances. As you wake up to the reality of the future and to the impact it has on your life, you realize that if you don't change the quality of your future, your life tomorrow will be the same as your life today.

By employing a few simple strategies you can give your future any quality you like. You can associate to it feelings of your choosing and can replace concepts that intimidate you with ones that empower you.

The effect of the future

The meaning you give to various aspects of your future is experienced as a positive or negative emotion. These in turn trigger patterns of action and reaction which set up the structuring causes for the circumstances of your life. Whether these emotions draw you along the path you have chosen or push you aside into the tangled, thorny underbrush that you are trying to avoid depends on how you set things up, internally.

No sailor can avoid the wind, but a wise one knows how to use it.

Getting information from the future

You are always getting information from the future. It is just as available to you as information from the past. It's just as accurate and just as influential. You haven't been aware of it because your beliefs have blinded you to it, but it plays an important role in your life. You couldn't plan a dinner party, pack for a summer vacation, solve a logistics problem or budget your money without first thinking of a possible future and asking yourself, What if ...? This question causes the mind to create the information you need to choose a course of action. The more conscious you are of the questions you ask yourself the more valuable this information becomes.

Harnessing the power of the future

A powerful leader gains influence because he creates a compelling vision of the future that motivates people to action. Successful individuals invariably create their own compelling vision. Then they harness its power to provide the information, inspiration and motivation necessary to achieve their goals. Remaining blind to the effect of a negative concept will leave you feeling victimized by the world when you are really victimizing yourself.

The future casts its shadow before it.

Knowing how to transform a negative thought form into a positive one allows you to harness the power of the future for your own purposes. This is the key to motivation and the key to success.

Cultivating a new reality

The future casts its shadow before it. Gardening involves first visualizing the results you want then planting seeds accordingly. The first shoots provide a foreshadow of the garden to come. It's the same with your life. Outer circumstances reflect inner cultivation. The work must precede the results. If you want happiness you must cultivate the necessary thinking. If you want success you must perform the necessary actions. You will only reap what you have already sown.

Cultivating a new reality involves making some fundamental decisions. Cultivating new physical circumstances involves mastering the Goals Process, a subject we'll cover in the next chapter. Cultivating a new personality means uncovering and eliminating your negative attitudes then cultivating a set of new, positive attitudes.

To eliminate a negative attitude your need to transform it into a positive one by changing the meaning of the reference events. We have already covered how to do this, but it's up to you to make the necessary changes. You need to take responsibility for your personality and for your world, then commit to investing the necessary effort. No one else can or will do it for you.

Cultivating happiness

It's a common belief that our feelings reflect our circumstances and that we'd feel better if our circumstances were different. This is untrue. Your level of happiness is simply a habit. It's no more the effect of your circumstances than voice tone is the effect of language. Both reflect deeper aspects of your consciousness.

If you think happiness is a function of your circumstances, you'll focus on trying to change your circumstances. But since the belief is false, no matter how much your circumstances change you'll feel no happier. You might even feel less happy, out of frustration.

Understand that happiness is a state of mind. To be happier you'll have to cultivate it. This is easily done. You begin by analyzing your current level of happiness and asking yourself these two questions:

> • *On a scale of ten, how happy am I today?*
> • *On a scale of ten, how happy would I like to be in the future?*

If the second number is higher than the first, you'll have to cultivate a new attitude about happiness by learning to feel happier in the present. Otherwise no matter what happens in the future you'll still feel disappointed.

The secret of happiness

At any moment there is as much to feel happy about as unhappy. Happiness ultimately comes down to two questions.

> What do you focus on?
> What meaning do you give it?

If you were to spend five minutes every morning and evening asking yourself the question, ***What do I have to feel happy about right now?*** you would notice lots to feel happy about. Over time this question would change your focus, your attitude and your feelings and your circumstances. It would cause your perceptions to change.

From your perspective, both your inner and your outer reality would have undergone a shift. You'd notice more things in the past to feel happy about. You'd notice more things in the present to feel happy about. You'd begin to expect greater happiness in the future, an expectation that would sow the seeds for a new level of happiness. The effort you put into changing your inner world would be reflected back to you, so whether or not there was any change in your circumstances, you'd feel better.

The law of growth

It takes time for a seed to become a full grown plant. It will take time for your new attitude to change your experience. Understanding this will alert you to small changes. Just as a gardener feels excited by seeing the first new shoots appearing in the Spring, you'll feel excited at the first hint of your new reality.

These two affirmations utilize the Law of Growth. They will alert you to the subtle changes taking place in your inner and outer worlds.

Two magic affirmations

The following two affirmations utilize the *Law of Growth*. They will alert you to the subtle changes taking place in your inner and outer worlds.

- I notice more _ *happiness* _ now.
- My life contains more things to be _*happy*_ about now.

These two affirmations effectively transform happiness from a *concept* existing in your mind into a tangible *aspect* of your present physical reality.

You can use them to cultivate any new emotion or attribute of your reality by filling in the first blank with *any positive emotion* and filling in the second with *any positive attribute*.

For example, if you wanted to increase your luck, you would simply say, 'I notice more luck now.' And 'I notice more things to feel lucky about now. '

- *Repeat these affirmations as often as possible.*
- *Write them on cards.*
- *Carry one with you and tape one to the dashboard of your car.*
- *Meditate on them for a few minutes in the morning and evening.*
- *Use the Affirmation Principle to erase any negative references they stimulate.*

The more often you repeat them the more alert you'll be to the many subtle positive changes occurring in your reality.

As you systematically cultivate the garden of your mind like this, you will experience more of the life you have chosen to enjoy. This marks the shift from *unconscious reacting* to *conscious creating*.

To watch a video on cultivating more blessings, or videos on other aspects of this book, go to my on-line blogs or You Tube site:

http://anthonysinsights.blogspot.com/
http://www.youtube.com/user/TonyinChina
http://www.path2success.org

Chapter Nineteen

Designing your Destiny

*You've got to have a dream.
If you don't have a dream,
how can you make your
dream come true?*

From a popular song

You were born with the power to create your dream life. But to access this power you need to know what your dream life is. You need to know its parts and how the parts fit together. When you fit all the pieces together you will have a mental image of the life you want to create for yourself.

I call this mental image, or concept, your 'Ideal Lifestyle'. It is your idea of the life you wish to create for yourself and to inhabit.

When you first begin to develop this mental picture, it will be vague, fuzzy and indistinct. However, over time it will become crystallized into a series of definite ideas representing the various aspects of your ideal life.

You next need to turn this vague ideas into a specific set of goals and specific action plans to achieve them.

Having a high degree of clarity about what you want to create for yourself enables you to focus the power of your mind like a laser, burning away obstacles and setting fire to the passion and the motivation you will need to create your ideal life.

But reaching this degree of mental clarity will take some time.

The mind moves from the general to the specific. In the beginning, having only a very vague idea of the life you want to create is quite natural.

The original concept for the movie 'Witness', starring Harrison Ford, was one sentence ... 'A Chicago cop befriends a little boy who witnesses a murder and becomes stranded in an Amish community.'

To expand this vague idea into the complete screenplay took the author ten years, even though the final script was only 110 pages long. Sometimes it takes time to get things exactly right.

A good way to approach the creation of your ideal lifestyle is to see the process as though you were writing a screenplay of the life you've always wanted.

You will start by making lists of what you want to do, to have or to be. Don't worry if your initial ideas are vague. Eventually all your goals and dreams will fit together perfectly.

It's a little like putting together a jig saw puzzle. At first you are not sure what the 'big picture' is. All the various pieces look more or less the same. Then, slowly, you can start to see what the various elements of the picture are, but not exactly how they fit together. Slowly, as you add more pieces to the puzzle, you start to see the 'big picture' and how it all fits together.

Don't worry if in the beginning you feel as though you were working in the dark. Clarity of vision and strength of purpose will come with practice. Take it one step at a time.

Here's what the process looks like.

Step one: stimulate your imagination

On each of ten file cards, write one of the following ten headings. Then write brief, one or two-word phrases of whatever comes to mind when you read the following instructions. Try for ten ideas on each card.

Likes: What gives you pleasure? What type of people do you enjoy being around? What type of work interests you? What do you like to do in your spare time? What have you always enjoyed doing? What have you done only rarely, that you would like to do more? What have you never done but think you'd like to?

- **Talents:** What talents do you *know* you have, *think you might have* or would like to have? What talents do you admire in others? What talents have you tried to develop but not been able to? What talents do others say you have? What talent would you prefer to have over all others? What talents do you think you have that you've never actually tried to develop?

- **Successes:** What have you always been good at? What wins have you had in the past? What things do you easily excel at? What seems natural to you? What have you never tried but think you could do easily?

- **Long-Range Goals:** What have you always wanted to accomplish? What has always been important to you? What goals have you promised yourself you will reach before you die? What things have you promised yourself you will avoid at all costs?

- **Childhood Dreams:** What roles did you imagine you would be playing as an adult? What situations did you see yourself in? Which did you tell yourself to avoid? Include all and any ideas that spring to mind when you place yourself mentally back in your childhood.

- **Reading:** What topics do you enjoy reading about? You might be an expert in something and not even be aware of it. List the main types of reading you engage in ... the main topics and authors.

- **Interests:** What always catches your attention? opera? horse racing? heroism? What themes do you like in movies? If you could watch an expert in some field perform, which would you choose? What activities have you been telling yourself you would like to study someday?

- **Fears:** What things are you *really* afraid of? Being alone? ... water? ... being rejected? ... heights? ... speaking in front of

142

people? ... success? ... failure? ... being different? ... being the same? ... power? ... weakness?

- **One Year to Live:** If you were going to die in a year, how would you feel? Experience the emotion. Then ask yourself what things you would do if you had only that much time left.

- **One Million Dollars:** If you had just won so much money that you'd have trouble spending the annual interest on it, what would you do? Take singing and dancing lessons? Travel? Write poetry? Get involved in charity work or in helping the handicapped? Put the main ideas down on this page.

Step two: record your mental snapshots

Once you have the cards filled out, read them over at least twice each day, soaking and bathing your mind in these ten categories of ideas. Carry them with you in our pocket or purse so they are available to read at odd moments ... sitting in traffic, waiting for a meal in a restaurant, standing in line at the grocery store. This gets your unconscious mind working below the surface,

 stimulating your imagination to give you lots of great ideas. When you least expect it you will experience a "mental snapshot" ... a fleeting glimpse of some part of your Fantasy Lifestyle.

Thomas Edison said, Ideas come from space. Broadcaster Earl Nightingale says, Good ideas are like slippery fish. If you don't gaff them with the end of a pencil, they'll slip away forever. Every creative person has learned to harness the creative power of the mind like this.

Record your mental snapshots on a page in your journal called a *Master Dream List*. The more mental snapshots you have on this list the better. These parts of your Fantasy Lifestyle may eventually become long and short-range goals you will choose to bring into existence.

Always have a small note pad and a pen in your pocket, in your car and beside your bed at night. When an idea pops into your head, write it down and transfer it to your Master Dream List. As they accumulate, these snapshots of your Fantasy Lifestyle will become clearer, with greater detail.

Include on your Master Dream List every thought you have concerning the life you want to live. Hold nothing back. Let no thought of limitation inhibit the free flow of ideas, even those that seem impossible.

Step three: divide your dreams into six categories

When you have a long list of dreams on your Master Dream List, separate them into six categories:

- ➢ Physical
- ➢ Mental
- ➢ Emotional
- ➢ Spiritual
- ➢ Social
- ➢ Financial

These six areas of your life are like six parts of your garden on which you will be concentrating your creative energies. Include a list of the feelings, emotions and personality traits you expect to be significant attributes of your new lifestyle. Eventually you will be setting goals in these areas, so hold nothing back.

Step four: prioritize your dreams

Take each of your six lists of dreams and prioritize them. Place the most exciting ones at the top. Take the top five dreams in each area and write them on six file cards, giving you your favorite thirty dreams in all six areas.

Place these six file cards side by side on your dining room table and sit quietly for several minutes. Look them over. Search for common patterns. Repeat this exercise on a daily basis, shuffling the cards each time. Your mind will respond with a series of mental snapshots of various lifestyles incorporating varying numbers of these dreams. Continue until one day, out of the blue, you experience a very special flash of insight, a vivid glimpse of a life that brings all your dreams together. This is a very special moment. It is your first image of your fantasy lifestyle.

A note of caution

This process that I just described in a few pages, can have some profound effects on your feelings, your emotions and your thinking.

When I did this exercise a number of years ago, I did it consistently for about 90 days before I got my first, big, 'AHA' moment.... my first breakthrough idea. But I had a lot of smaller 'aha's' before that.

You may find yourself having dreams, in which you are living parts of your new ' fantasy lifestyle'. You may get flashes of ideas for new careers, new relationships, new possible ways of living your life that either inspire you and fill you with energy, or fill you with doubt, uncertainty and feelings of unworthiness.

Try not to get emotionally caught up in these feelings. Just record the ideas that come to you and continue to contemplate the cards and pages in your journal. Eventually everything will become clear.

Give yourself time to experience the change in thinking that this exercise will stimulate in you.

Chapter Twenty

The Goals Process

*Those with no goals are destined
to follow those who do.*

Paul Low

On a scale of 1-10, how successful are you right now? On the same scale, how successful would you like to be in the future?

If you want more success in the future than you have now you'll have to understand what success is and how to cultivate it.

The word 'success' belongs to the same family of words as *succession* and *successive*. It implies a step-by-step process as in, 'The line of succession went from the father to the son to the grandson.'

Earl Nightingale defines success as 'The progressive realization of a worthy ideal'. According to this definition, being successful requires two things: 1. That you have a dream, an idea. 2. That you be *in the process* of turning your dream into reality.

In the last chapter I outlined a system that would help you  define your dream. I gave instructions for creating it as a concept in your mind called your **Ideal Lifestyle**.

Anything you want more of in life forms part of this concept. Therefore, being successful comes down to being **in the process** of transforming your Ideal Lifestyle into physical reality. And isn't this exactly what you want?

Notice that in the previous paragraph I emphasized the phrase, 'in the process'. This is because you must actually be in the process of doing the exercises for the ideas to have any effect.

If you are walking from point 'a' to point 'b' you are *doing something* that will eventually get you to point 'b'. However, if you are merely thinking of going to point 'b' you will never get there... until you start walking. This is what I mean by being *in the process*.

The process of creating your dream begins by making the commitment to experience it. This commitment transforms the dream into a goal and marks the beginning of the Goals Process.

Success is defined as the action of engaging in the Goals Process.

The physical manifestation of your dream is the by-product of this course of action. Therefore cultivating success comes down to using the Goals Process to bring your mental model of the future into your present reality as a physical part of it.

Like a gardener watching more and more shoots appearing in his garden, when you engage in this process you will progressively experience more parts of your Ideal Lifestyle appearing in your life as aspects of physical reality.

The key to the Goals Process is to understand what a goal is.

A goal is a possibility you have committed to experiencing.

Many people think they have goals when they don't. They only have preferences. Misunderstanding the distinction between the two will rob you of your power.

A goal is something you are committed to experiencing. A preference is merely a conditional desire. With a preference you are really telling yourself, I'd like to have this in my life if it doesn't take too much work. With a preference your level of intention depends on external conditions, meaning you are giving your power away to something outside of yourself. Committing to a goal means you are willing to do whatever it takes to create it. This places the point of power within your control.

Most people will give up on a preference after one or two attempts, giving themselves no real opportunity for success. They'll tell themselves they failed because external obstacles prevented

147

them, when in truth what stopped them was not external but internal.

When you commit to a goal external circumstances become transformed from obstacles into conditions which need to be dealt with. Making a commitment moves your mind to a different level of intention. It galvanizes your mind into focusing all its resources on creating the desired goal.

Characteristics of a goal

A goal is distinguished by five characteristics.

- It is clearly-defined.
- You are committed to reaching it.
- You have a time limit for reaching it.
- You have an action plan for reaching it.
- You are acting on your plan today.

If any of these five characteristics is missing you don't have a goal but a preference. Your level of desire will not be strong enough to create it. You need to transform your preference into a goal.

Preference → Goal

Transforming a preference into a goal

To transform your preference into a goal you need to:

> Commit to experiencing it.
>
> Design a step-by-step plan of action.
>
> Follow your plan every day until you have achieved the goal.

A model of conscious goal-creation

Let's say my goal is to attend a meeting in San Francisco at a certain time on a certain date and my plan is to drive there from my home in Vancouver.

Achieving the goal involves the process of driving from point A to point B in a certain time. There are countless ways I could achieve the goal. When I set out from Vancouver I begin the process  and I maintain the process by making a series of choices and performing a series of actions.

When I first set out the choices I make are very general. I need only be driving South to be doing the right thing.

But as I get closer to my destination, my choices become progressively more precise and must be made in the correct order. Eventually I will arrive at a specific building, take an elevator to a specific floor and walk into a specific room at a specific time. At this point I have achieved my goal and the process comes to an end.

There are several key points to note in this example. The first is that although my goal is achieved as I walk into the room, I am successful as soon as I begin the process and continue to be successful as long as I maintain the process.

The second is that each point along the route is an intermediate goal, with my ultimate destination simply the last in a series.

The third is that the process involves continuously modifying  my actions in light of current circumstances. If my car breaks down, I'm still successful sitting in a coffee shop waiting for the repairs to be made. I don't cease being successful just because I have to modify my plan. This illustrates the fact that success is a <u>byproduct</u> of my actions not the <u>result</u> of them.

People who misunderstand this distinction link success to results and results to actions. This leads to increasing stress and frustration when my actions don't lead to the desired results. Worse yet, they run the risk of giving up all together after one or two unsuccessful attempts. This mind set practically guarantees their dream will never materialize.

Understand that results are never guaranteed. What worked yesterday might lead to totally unexpected results today.

By maintaining your commitment to the process and modifying your actions in light of present conditions, you make the eventual manifestation of your goal increasingly certain. Unforeseen circumstances can only slow you down. Nothing can prevent your success but you.

The secret of my success

To explain my success from a Newtonian perspective an observer would have to say my success was due to my starting point and caused by my actions along the way. To explain how I could predict the eventual outcome, he'd have to invent a reason. He might say it was a lucky guess or that perhaps I was psychic, since from his perspective knowing the future is impossible.

But do I have a special psychic gift? Did I come from someplace special? Did I do anything unique? Do I possess special talent? Am I blessed by some mysterious accident of genetics? Of course not. I succeeded for four reasons:

> I knew my point of origin and my destination.
>
> I had a map with clear checkpoints.
>
> I had a time line and a watch to provide feedback.
>
> I was constantly engaged in a process of modifying my actions relative to my progress.

Achieving my goal was the by-product of this process. Any attempt to explain the outcome in terms of my point of origin or my actions is doomed. Both are meaningful only in terms of my overall plan. Because I was prepared to speed up, slow down or change direction at any time, I knew achieving my goal was certain as long as I maintained the process.

The secret of your success

The secret of your success will be to plan your life and live your plan.

You need to decide what you want out of life and formulate a strategy for creating it.

Success has nothing to do with where you come from and everything to do with *where you are going*. It has nothing to do with *talent* or *luck*. It has little to do with your *actions* and everything to do with the *timing and arrangement* of your actions.

You can be successful regardless of your past. You need no special skills. The actions you need to perform to achieve your goals have been performed by millions before you and are currently being performed by thousands of people in your very own city.

To cultivate success you need only *clarify your goal, formulate your plan* and *structure your actions* accordingly.

We all know people who are going in circles and don't know why. They are driving hard but making no progress. They are busy but not effective. They don't know where they are or where they're going.

They react to events they don't understand and over which they have no control. They are not decisive. They are not motivated. They have no power and no enthusiasm. They will follow anyone who looks like he knows where he's going. They are the blind following the blind, living lives of quiet desperation. They are destined to get stuck in the same ruts as the people they're following.

These people live in the hope they'll get lucky. They hope to eventually find themselves in a *place called success* where they will be *happy*. But almost inevitably they'll find themselves in a place they didn't choose and don't want because they never took the time to plan their life and live their plan.

They'll blame their lack of success on *external circumstances*. They'll think life has done it to them when they have really *done it to themselves*. When all is said and done, and you are enjoying the results of your planning and your commitment to the *success process*, these people will be sitting on the side of the road out of gas.

 Don't you make this mistake. Commit to using the *Goals Process* to systematically transform your dreams into your reality.

How to achieve any goal

Once you learn to drive and read a map, you can travel anywhere using the same basic skills. The first time you get a flat you may need help to change the tire, but the second time you'll be able to manage on your own. It's the same in life.

The Goals Process is the master principle leading to the level of power, success and happiness you desire. When your pattern of thinking, feeling and acting has become modularized through daily application of the Goals Process you'll automatically do what's

152

necessary to keep yourself on track and on target. You'll have moved from unconsciously creating what you don't want to unconsciously creating what you do. Your outer life will reflect your inner harmony and sense of power. The circumstances you desire will blossom around you like a garden coming into flower in the Spring. Others may say you are lucky, but you'll know the truth. Your success is a byproduct of maintaining the Goals Process.

Like any process, parts of the Goals Process can be viewed in isolation appearing to be a series of cause-and-effect actions. But the secret lies in maintaining the process, not performing the actions. Here's how to use the Goals Process to achieve any goal:

Step one: Gathering information

Choose a dream from some area of your Ideal Lifestyle you can commit to. This commitment transforms it into a goal. Using this as a reference point, take a few sheets of paper. Label each of them with one of these headings, Assets, Liabilities, Where Do I Stand Now? and What's It Worth to Me? Fill them out like this:

Assets. List all your strengths, talents and assets. Put down everything you are good at, everything you enjoy doing and everything you feel you have a knack for. Don't be concerned if you can't see how these assets might be used. Just write them down.

Liabilities. List everything you consider a physical, emotional, mental, financial or social liability.

Where Do I Stand Now? Write an essay describing your life today in relation to your goal, listing the positive and negative attributes in this area of your life. For the positive attributes ask, How could I increase the value of this attribute? For the negative, How could I decrease the liability caused by this attribute? Strive for objectivity.

What's It Worth to Me? List all the reasons why achieving this goal is important to you. Knowing your reasons for acting is vitally important. This list will become increasingly valuable later on as you encounter resistance and need to recommit to your goal. Many people make a basic mistake of forgetting why their goal is important, causing them to give up. To stop doing something that benefits your life because you've forgotten your reasons for doing so is a tragedy. Don't fall into this trap

Step two: Create a plan of action and a time line.

Decide on a date by which you plan to achieve your goal. Break it down to a series of steps and assign each an intermediate date. Sketch out where you'll need to be at the 25%, 50%, 75% mark. This is only a rough sketch. You'll be modifying and refining this plan as you go.

Step three: Take a step in the right direction.

Read the sheets from step one and do what's necessary to complete the next step in your plan. If it seems too big, break it down further to a series of even smaller steps. Taking action engages you in the Goals Process, making you successful by definition. It also starts bringing aspects of your goal into the present.

Step four: Evaluate your progress.

Ask yourself this series of questions:

- What specific outcome am I committed to?
- Where am I now in relation to this outcome?
- What do I need to do today to move me closer to my goal?
- What am I doing that's working?
- What am I doing that's not working?
- What attitude will empower me to act?
- What attitude will make me feel good about what's happening right now?

These questions will keep you in control of your emotions, your focus, your actions and your life.

Step Five: Go back to step three.

Reread the sheets from step one and take the next step in your plan. Walking is a process of continuously losing and regaining your balance. At any point you can fall over, but once you learn to get back up and regain your balance you can go anywhere. The five steps in this process will take you from where you are now to wherever you wish to go. Master them and your life will be transformed.

Organizing your great ideas

Your Plan of Action is an organizing principle. Reading it over stimulates your mind to create specific information, making it respond with a steady stream of valuable ideas, many coming at odd, unexpected moments. By writing them down and organizing them, you'll create a priceless resource to help you create the life of your choice. You'll soon discover that these ideas fall into several categories, but if you don't develop a filing system for organizing them you'll miss out on the help they can offer you.

Some ideas will be about the present, detailing possible action steps. Some will be names of people to call, books to read or courses to take. Others will be intuitive ways of dealing with problem situations you are facing or will soon need to handle. Another category of ideas will be about the past. These can be memories of past successes, when you achieved goals similar to the one you are currently working on. Others will be memories of mistakes you've made that you'll want to avoid making again. These memories can provide you with priceless information and insight. Still other ideas will be about the future, perhaps ideas of the benefits you anticipate enjoying as a result of achieving the goal.

All these ideas can be very valuable to you. Each will have its use. But if you don't have a way or organizing them they'll get lost in a jumble and be of no value to you. Here's what I recommend: Take several sheets of paper and label them, Action Steps, Situations, Possible Solutions, Past Successes, Benefits to Me.

Organize these sheets in your binder and use them to record these ideas as they come to you. Since many ideas will pop into your head at unexpected times, carry a note pad with you to write them down, transferring them to this filing system later.

Label another sheet, Affirmations. On this sheet you will record statements you feel would be valuable for uncovering negative references or which you can develop into positive attitudes using the Affirmation Principle.

Establish a daily routine

The French word for day is jour. This is the origin of the word journey and the word journal. The process of creating your dream means living one day at a time. Imagine yourself on a journey from where you are now to where you want to be, living each day with purpose and recording your progress in your journal. This attitude increases your effectiveness and keeps you in conscious control of the process until the conditions you desire have been created.

Use your journal to record insights gained from working with the Affirmation Principle. Use it to clarify your plan of action and to organize the ideas you are using as building blocks to create your new life.

Use your journal to track your feelings, emotions and beliefs as you weed out thoughts that tend to hold you back and cultivate those that tend to move you ahead. Applying your efforts where they will have the most effect will keep you on track and on time. The result of your efforts will be a life that works.

Decide on a specific time each day when you can spend fifteen minutes or so working in this journal, transferring ideas from your note pad onto one of the lists I just described, or refining your Plan of Action.

As you continue the process of taking daily action steps, use your Time Line as a guide to assess your progress. Continue modifying your actions as needed. By working your plan on a daily basis, you'll form the habit of living the Goals Process as a definite lifestyle. You'll remain conscious of where you are, where you are going and what conditions must be dealt with each step of the way. Deal with each unforeseen circumstance as an intermediate goal. The mental snapshots that come to you in ever increasing numbers will demonstrate to you in no uncertain terms that your subconscious mind is working with you as an active partner, helping to create the life of your dreams. Let others stand on the sidelines complaining about the past, feeling victimized by the present or worried about the future. You have work to do.

Staying on the path

If simply putting a plan into action guaranteed results, everyone would be rich, happy and successful. Problems arise because our conception of what the route will be like from here to there is not real. It is a thought form, a generalization. Like a mental map of the city in which you life, much of the information it contains is distorted and false. Other information is simply missing. You may  drive the same route to work each day, but don't know how many houses you pass on the way. Perhaps you can't even name the streets you pass on a daily basis.

In moving into the future, we can't foresee the exact conditions we'll encounter or predict the exact results of our actions. We only discover these as we go. Many times we end up in situations we did not foresee. What do we do when unforeseen circumstances side-track us or bog us down?

In *Unlimited Power*, Anthony Robbins clearly shows that the difference between success and failure is to maintain the Goals Process no matter what. The key to staying on the path when the going gets tough, is to realize that only two things can interfere with our progress, unforeseen external circumstances and our own negative feelings. Both can be dealt with when we cultivate the correct attitude.

You can deal with any unexpected external condition by incorporating it as an intermediate step in your Plan of Action.

157

Avoid the trap of believing that it's unique to your situation. Realize instead that all men and women of achievement have faced similar circumstances and that thousands of people are dealing with virtually identical conditions today. Some will be successful, some not. This attitude brings the external condition down to size. It eliminates the feeling that you are fighting the battle alone and helps overcome the urge to quit. Don't let your unconscious reaction to an unexpected situation side-track you. Go back to your journal. Write another, "Where do I stand now?" essay. Keep moving.

Dealing with negative feelings always involves handling fear, a subject I cover in the next chapter. At this point just remember the bottom line. If we let fear stop us from completing any step in our plan, the process comes to a halt and we have down-graded our goal to a preference. We have given our power away by letting some imagined condition intimidate us. Remember that any imagined situation is only a thought. Your power is only one thought away. Accept responsibility for the attitudes, the beliefs and the concepts which are the structuring cause for your feelings. Search for the frame of reference that transforms it from a negative thought into a positive one. You will find it.

To deal with negative feelings, ask yourself, What exactly am I feeling? Then ask, What attitudes are causing this feeling? and What attitude would make me feel good about what's happening right now?

Eliminate the negative attitudes by using the Affirmation Principle. By cultivating a new positive attitude and controlling your emotions, you empower yourself to take the next step. This series of questions is often all it takes to get back on track.

But make no mistake, dealing with fear takes skill, commitment, courage, and effort. Your ability to stay the course is tested at these times as you deal with the urge to quit. Recommit to your vision, your plan and your goal.

Re-commit to your goal

In his autobiography Benjamin Franklin described his method for making decisions. He took a sheet of paper, drew a line down the middle and on one side wrote, Benefits, on the other, Costs. He then made a long list of each to help him decide. This is how you will decide whether your goal is still worth the effort required to stay on track. When faced with an unforeseen situation that makes you want to quit, read your list of benefits. Imagine you have already achieved the goal and are enjoying these benefits in the present. Notice how you feel about being a winner.

Next, read your list of costs. What would it cost you to take another step toward the goal. Notice how you feel. Are the rewards worth the cost of taking the next step?

When you're stuck, this exercise will help you decide whether your goal is worth the effort required to stay on the path. In trying times you may have to recommit over and over again as you find yourself facing either internal or external conditions you didn't expect. Quite often you'll discover that what you really have to give up are your limiting beliefs and attitudes. This is intimidating. It takes skill. Rereading the lists you've written in Step One will help you over this hurdle.

The ability to continue taking steps, repeatedly modifying your plan in the face of unforeseen difficulties, is what separates those on the path from those sitting on the sidelines complaining. Expect the unexpected. No condition has any power over you but the power you give it by attaching a meaning to it. Remember that you only ever have to commit to maintaining the process for one more day. Live life one day at a time. Tomorrow things may be different.

When I was a young man I worked for a small mining company which eventually became very large. It didn't have the resources to invest years in a futile search for new ore bodies. So the owners of the company formulated a plan. They reasoned that if a large company with a lot of resources at its command thought drilling in a certain area was promising, the chances were good that there was an ore body near by. So they looked for a property that a large company had invested a lot of money in and given up on without finding anything. They took out an option on the property and hired some drillers to put their drill bits into the same holes the original owners were drilling into. They told the drillers to simply keep on drilling and when the drillers had gone only thirty feet farther, they came across a huge ore body the original owners would have discovered if they hadn't quit.

How will you feel if you give up on your dream and realize five years from now that you could have succeeded if only you'd carried on?

Cultivate persistence

The obstacles to your success are always internal, but so are your greatest assets. Reading your list of Past Successes will increase your confidence. Reading your list of expected benefits will increase your motivation. If you find yourself stuck at any step, redo the cost/benefit analysis. If you decide the goal really is worth it, carry on. Almost immediately things will begin to look better and you'll once again feel excited and motivated. If you try this you will discover the secret to tapping the great wellspring of creative power to which you are connected.

Transform your personality

Remembering that external conditions are a reflection of your inner self, the question you need to ask is not, What do I need to do? but, Who do I need to become?

Monitor your emotions, your attitudes and your beliefs on an ongoing basis. Realize you are not the same person who started the journey. You are being transformed by the process of creating your dream. You will experience the creation of your Ideal Lifestyle not as a series of goals you are achieving, but as a reflection of the new personality you are creating.

As you develop insight into what is really important, your understanding of your life will change. You will experience more joy, more freedom, more peace of mind and more success. You will feel less like a passenger on your ship of fate and more like the captain. You will know where you are, where you are going and how to get there. Remind yourself of the great progress you've already made. Anticipate even greater results in the days to come. Continue the process.

Designing your life

No carpenter would build a house without first drawing up a detailed set of plans. To do so would guarantee a house riddled with structural defects. Heat would leak out. Water would leak in. Time, energy and money would be wasted patching and repairing the place.

Lyle Hamer, a good friend of mine who's a master carpenter, recently built a house for his family on a beautiful island off the coast of British Columbia. Before construction began he and his wife Shelly planned the house out in exquisite detail. They made drawings showing every door, window and structural piece. They knew exactly how much wood, how many pieces of pipe, brick and drywall they would need. They even knew how many nails and screws they would eventually require. They did all this before they began to build. Lyle even made a cardboard model of the house to see how it would look when finished.

During the actual construction of the house, Lyle engaged in a series of actions. He measured, cut, hammered and assembled. These same actions could just as easily have resulted in the construction of a barn, a fence or a huge pile of lumber nailed together in a heap. The reason a house resulted was that Lyle's actions took place in a specific context. He didn't build his family's home by cutting wood and hammering nails. He did it by organizing his cutting and hammering according to a plan. His actions and his plan worked together, each providing feedback for the other. The house that resulted was a product of the overall process.

My arrival at the San Francisco meeting is clearly the result of a process, not the effect of simply pressing my foot on the gas pedal and the brake and turning the wheel back and forth. Without the feedback provided by my map and my watch, these behaviors would never have gotten me there on time. In driving from here to there, in building a home or in creating a life, actions alone will never produce what you want. Without a plan around which you organize your actions, you risk straying off course without even knowing it.

Mastering the goals process will enable you to achieve any goal, but without a balanced plan for your life as a whole, you may awake one day to find the goals you have been pursuing have thrown your life off balance. You don't want that. With a balanced plan all your efforts have a greater purpose and the goals you achieve today will enhance every area of your life. Make sure you have a balanced set of goals in every area of your life. Follow your plan. Make every day a success and the ultimate creation of your Ideal Lifestyle is guaranteed.

When I created my Ideal Lifestyle I had a coordinated set of dreams for all areas of my life. I pretended I was working on a screenplay of my future and I continued to refine it. If I came up with a better idea than one I'd already written down, I replaced it. My commitment to doing this on a daily basis has lead to a habit I have maintained to this day and which has given my life a quality I couldn't put a price on. Along the way I have gained great insight into myself. I have developed strength of mind, clarity of vision and a sense of purpose. I have developed patience and persistence. I've learned how to plan a course of action and how to stick to it. I've learned how to remain motivated no matter what the circumstances, how to remain calm in the face of difficulty and how to feel successful when it doesn't look like I'll ever achieve my goals. One of my early Dream Lists contained the line, "Write a book". At the time it seemed like an impossible dream, but you are holding in your hands one result of pursuing this idea.

My commitment to spending at least a few minutes each day designing and balancing my life has returned the small investment many thousands of times over.

I sincerely suggest you make the same commitment.

162

Create a blueprint for your life

Most people spend less time planning their lives than planning a two-week vacation. They waste energy doing things which are not moving them in the right direction. They have no power. Different areas of their life compete with each other for attention, sapping their energy. They may be driving hard but they  aren't going anywhere. They may be working hard but they aren't building anything. They haven't taken the time to look squarely at themselves and ask two basic questions: "What do I want out of life?" and "Am I committed to doing what's necessary to bring it about?"

My blueprint consists of a three ring binder, some loose leaf paper and some dividers. I separate it into two main sections. One is called, Goals and Action Plans. The other is called Attitudes, Beliefs and Emotions. The first is for organizing my outer world. The second my inner world.

I have further divided the Goals and Action Plans section into five areas; Physical, Mental, Spiritual, Financial, and Relationships. In each section I have a Dream List, and lists entitled, Possible Goals, Goals, Goals Already Reached, What It's Worth to Me, Conditions, Solutions, Plan of Action, Beliefs, Affirmations and Progress so Far. Each section is further divided into Long Range and Short Range dreams and goals. I've found that each of these categories of ideas has a particular purpose and that it's important to be able to locate them at specific times. I suggest you create a binder modeled after mine.

Just as Lyle's blueprint for his family's home covered every detail of his future home, your blueprint will cover every detail of the life you are creating.

163

In the opening chapter I spoke of a magical process incorporating five interwoven themes - Motivation, Attitude, Goals, Imagination and Consciousness.

This process is the Goals Process, expanded to cover every facet of your Ideal Lifestyle. Choosing goals in every area of your life and developing a coordinated set of action plans will give you great insight and clarity of mind. Over time, as you define your priorities and balance one goal against another, you'll come to understand where to focus your energy.

Put some effort into clarifying your vision of your Ideal Lifestyle on a daily basis. Choose individual parts of it as possible goals and do the Cost/Benefit analysis on them. This helps you decide whether you should make a commitment to achieving them. As you clarify your vision you are more able to use your imagination effectively. By sending your inner awareness to a chosen goal and experiencing it in your imagination, it becomes a source of information, inspiration and motivation, enabling you to plan effective actions to bring it about. As you continue this process your awareness expands, shedding more light into the shadows of your unconscious mind, increasing your power and effectiveness.

The daily habit of clarifying your goals, developing your plans and working with your attitudes and emotions will give you a level of understanding, confidence and power unknown to the average person. With increased clarity comes the ability to ask ever more specific questions and make progressively more informed choices. You will soon find yourself creating opportunities for realizing what you desire.

You'll come to realize that your Ideal Lifestyle already exists and is already affecting you. The inner reality of it generates a cosmic wind that can carry you along. It calls to you from a specific inner space-time location. By tapping into it with the pipeline of your imagination you extract from it the information you need to make the decisions that will guarantee your safe arrival.

When I first began the process of designing my life, I set up a binder like the one I am describing here and asked myself, Is taking charge of my life important enough for me to use this system every day? My answer was Yes. So I began filling out the sheets, writing the essays and working in my binder. I gained lots of insight and began achieving my goals. I was making progress, thinking more clearly and feeling great.

Some weeks later I awoke feeling tired, confused and stuck. (Just like old times!) My new-found confidence had faded. Then I realized it had been weeks since I had opened my binder. I'd gotten so caught up in the day-to-day activities of my life I had stopped doing the very things that had been making the difference. As soon as I realized this I made two minor corrections. I made a list of reasons why working in my binder was important and I promised myself that if nothing else, I'd at least open my binder every day and read this list. As soon as I returned to my binder work, things once again began to happen. Ideas started popping into my head. Insights began coming to me. I gained a clearer picture of the life I wanted to create and remained conscious of my reasons for wanting it. I began once again moving ahead in my life. I was back on track. I sincerely invite you to do the same.

Chapter Twenty One

The Key to Self-Motivation

Good and evil, reward and punishment,
are the only motives to a rational creature.
These are the spur and reins whereby
all mankind are set on work, and guided.

John Locke

The pinnacle of the magician's art is to consciously control the transformation of an idea into a living thing; to move your dream from your private world of thought where only you experience it to the outer world where others experience it as a physical reality along with you. When you identify the main parts of your Fantasy Lifestyle and have a list of the goals you must reach to create it, a direction and a path will make itself clear to you. It is your job to place yourself upon this path and remain on it until you have arrived at the destination you seek.

The overall process can be looked at two ways, actively or passively. The active aspect means putting energy into creating the physical world we desire. The passive aspect means allowing ourselves to be included in something which already exists. When I drive to San Francisco, I don't need to create the city. It's already there. I need only decide to do what's necessary to become a part of it. If I want more love in my life I don't need to create people who love me. They already exist. I need only be willing to be one of the people who experiences their love; to become a part of their circle. Thinking passively means cultivating the belief system that allows us to experience the life of our dreams as a reflection of who we are; to focus our efforts on allowing the world we desire to find us.

166

You must embark on both an inner and an outer journey, knowing that along the way you will need to deal with both internal and external conditions you never expected and might have thought impossible. The key ingredient to experiencing your dream as a thing rather than an idea is to take action, and the key to action is motivation. Without sufficient motivation you will never begin your journey or remain motivated long enough to cross the finish line. The purpose of this chapter is to give you the tools to set yourself on course and remain on course until you physically experience the realization of your dream.

What is motivation?

The word motivation seems to be made up of the two words *motive* and *action*. A good way to think of motivation is in terms of action and the motives for action. All action is preceded by a choice and the reasons for your choice are both conscious and unconscious. The car you drive was probably purchased as the result of primarily conscious choices. But what about your body? your health? your income? your emotions? your degree of happiness? your personality? your self-image? your relationships? Any area of your life that is not what you want means it is the result of a series of mostly unconscious choices; the effect of beliefs, attitudes, emotions and concepts of which you are unaware. To consciously change your reality you must become more aware of the unconscious choices you are making and make more conscious ones.

The two kinds of motivation

There are only two kinds of motivation: ***external*** (motivation by others) and ***internal*** (self-motivation). When your boss says, *If you increase your production next month, I'll give you a bonus.* This is motivation through *incentive*. When he says, *If you don't increase your production next month, you won't be getting a paycheque*, this is motivation through a *threat*. These two make up the carrot and stick approach to external motivation, and are the only form of motivation we encounter in our daily affairs.

If you require external motivation to achieve your goals you are giving your power away. You are like a sailor waiting for a wind that never comes, since others will only attempt to motivate you to achieve their goals, not yours. If you are waiting for someone else to push you toward your goals, you will never succeed. To consciously create your life you must master the art of self-motivation.

The two keys to self-motivation

To be self-motivated we must know exactly *what* we want. To sustain our efforts in the face of resistance we must know precisely *why* we want it. To recommit to the goal we must remain conscious of both this what and this why. Most people can't do this; their thinking is simply too muddled. Being self-motivated means thinking clearly, acting with purpose and persevering.

You already have the knowledge required to give yourself the what. Working in your binder will clarify your goals to a greater degree than most people ever experience and refining your plan of action will tell you exactly what choices you need to make to bring your goals about. Motivating yourself to make these choices will require a strong why. Developing this why is the topic of the rest of this chapter.

Two pillars support this why ... *desire* and *belief*. Each has a dual nature. To cultivate self-motivation you need to understand how these four aspects interact with each other in your mind and in your body.

The First Key - Desire

The two aspects of desire are the desire to experience what you want and the desire to avoid what you don't want. The first can be called, a goal, a want, a wish, a passion, a craving, a fancy or a leaning. The second can be called a hate, a repulsion or an aversion, but all are simply other names for fear. The main reason you are not already living your dream is that your fear of placing yourself on the path and staying there is stronger than your desire. While you set about cultivating a strong desire, you need to uproot the fear of acting and replace it with the fear of not acting. This means confronting your fear and developing its antidotes ... courage, persistence and self-confidence.

Creating desire

You must create and maintain a consistently high level of desire for the results you want. When no one else believes in your dream, when your friends are telling you to give up, to stop being so hard on yourself, to be realistic; only a strong desire will keep you moving in the right direction. To follow your friends' urgings means giving up on your dream and allowing yourself to be absorbed into theirs. Which choice will you make?

The bottom line is that desire is a state you can create and maintain, as already explained. You must learn to create this state when you want it, increase it when necessary and sustain it as long as required. The strength of your desire depends on the value of the benefits you expect balanced against the price you will pay for them. The greater the benefit of winning and the cost of losing, the stronger your desire. It's that simple.

The first step in cultivating your desire is to write down the expected benefits using the *What's it Worth to Me?* sheet in your binder. Reading this list will increase your desire and help motivate you to overcome your inertia. Reading a second list of the costs of not acting will help motivate you to keep taking action. Work both sides of the process.

The Second Key - Belief

The second pillar of self-motivation is belief. It too is a state, which can be generated, sustained and modified, as previously discussed. It also has two aspects; belief *that* and belief *how*. You must believe that your dream is possible or you will never attempt it. If this aspect of your belief is weak you won't be able to sustain your motivation over the long haul. If you need other people to believe in your goal before you can believe in it yourself you are giving your power away. To keep putting one foot in front of the other you must cultivate a strong belief that achieving your vision is possible.

Your level of motivation is also affected by your unique pattern of belief concerning how your vision will be realized. If you believe achieving your goal will take a lot of hard work over a long period of time your mind will automatically filter *in* ideas that involve working hard for a long period of time and blind you to ideas of how you might create it easily and quickly. If someone tells you of a way you could reach your goal without doing a lot of hard work, it won't *feel* right. You'll feel uncomfortable because the idea will conflict with your belief in how things work. You'll tell yourself things like, *It must be illegal, It can't be that simple, There must be more to it than that,* and dismiss the idea. This will make you feel better because you will have erased your inner conflict. You'll have a good reason, but you won't have your dream.

If the effort involved in creating your dream exactly how you expect becomes too much your belief will be weakened. You'll think the opposition you feel is coming from the world, but it will really be coming from inside you. This aspect of your belief is very subtle and will take constant journal work to uncover. You'll need to pay close attention to your feelings and carefully analyze the beliefs that trigger them, weeding out those that cause difficulty and cultivating those that empower you. Your best tool for doing this is the Affirmation Principle. By working with it on a daily basis you will become increasingly conscious of the contents of your mind and will gain great insight into how your beliefs are focusing your thoughts, perceptions, feelings and behavior.

Motivation, desire and belief are related this way:

Level of Motivation = Desire x Belief

Inner conflict

Your level of motivation depends on the strength of both your desire and your belief. If either is nonexistent you'll have no motivation no matter how strong the other. If either is out of alignment with your goals and purpose internal conflict will either destroy your motivation altogether or create neurotic behavior patterns. You'll need to watch yourself closely to discover these patterns and analyze your belief system to discover where the conflict lies. This depth of internal examination requires uncommon insight and courage.

You'll know something is going on with you when you find yourself repeatedly starting toward a goal only to give up halfway, or feeling unsatisfied when you accomplish something you thought would make you happy. Having a strong desire for a goal you simultaneously feel you don't deserve will create tremendous internal conflict. Likewise, if you believe achieving your goal involves doing things that are unethical your subconscious mind will resist you every step of the way. Conflicting beliefs cause you to constantly fight yourself, causing a level of discomfort (dis-ease) that not only creates tension in your body and confusion in your mind, but also makes uncomfortable those with whom you interact.

When you find yourself continually hampered by petty annoyances like this your desire to be successful will be replaced by feelings of anger, frustration, disappointment and resentment. You'll project your internal conflict onto the world, blaming it for your problems, concluding the world is against you, that you have bad luck, or that it's your destiny to live a life of lack. But the resistance you think you are experiencing in the world will be an illusion. The real culprit is not external but internal. Such a situation indicates something else is going on. This something else is fear. To remain on track and on purpose you'll have to deal with it.

Dealing with fear

In plain language, fear is the expectation of pain. But an intense fear is a strong, negative conviction that entangles your body and mind in a gruesome dance of confused thinking, painful emotions and convoluted logic. Fear causes your imagination to draw images of painful situations from the possible future, triggering painful feelings you'll try anything to avoid. Problems arise when you have

171

unconsciously associated these negative feelings to some of the steps in your action plan. Following your plan without untangling these associations forces you into a confrontation with your fears, tying your mind into knots.

As previously discussed, association is an automatic function of the mind. If you unconsciously associate pain to a behavior, you'll put off doing it without knowing why. You'll just tell yourself you *don't feel like* doing it. (This is why people resist going to the dentist.) But if the action you're putting off is part of your plan, your forward motion will cease and you'll become one of those people I wrote of earlier; driving hard but not going anywhere. By avoiding following your plan you involve yourself in a cycle of frustration and failure that can easily cause you to give up on your goal if you're not careful. Only when the pain of continuing to avoid taking action becomes stronger than the pain of not taking it will you break out of this cycle. (When the tooth aches bad enough you call the dentist!) To break free of this cycle consciously without wasting a lot of time or energy requires doing the necessary work to analyze your conceptual framework, your belief system and your plan of action, rearranging the unconscious associations so they work for you rather than against you. To do this inner work effectively takes uncommon courage and skill.

Taking action on your plan sets up the structuring cause for the creation of your dream; not acting implies that you don't want it. If you're so afraid of getting *tails* that you won't flip the coin, you'll never get *heads*. When you procrastinate you force your dream to remain a virtual reality that never materializes. Your unconscious, fear-based choices create the exact situation you've consciously been trying to avoid by setting up the structuring cause for the situation which would exist if you had no desire for your goal. Procrastination is telling the universe, *I don't want my dream to come true*. This downgrades your goal to a preference and moves it from a potential position on your world line into the realm of impossible dreams. When you procrastinate you abandon your dream for someone else to experience. Is that what you want?

The emotional pain that causes procrastination is a function of the way you have unconsciously designed your Plan of Action, associating a meaning to some of the steps that makes you expect pain. These expected negative feelings can range from mild irritation and embarrassment to absolute terror or disgust; from the fear of ridicule to the certainty you'll never again be able to show your face. If these feelings stop you from completing any step, you negate all your previous efforts. This would be like driving all the way to San Francisco and being afraid to enter the meeting room. The net effect would be the same as if you had never left home.

The bad news is that the emotional pain stopping you is the same pain that's been stopping you all your life, meaning it is very deeply embedded in your body and mind. It is the last thing you want to look at. The good news is that once you identify it and erase it, it will never stop you again. You'll be free to create your dreams unhampered by a fear that's controlled you all your life. Many people never escape these unconscious traps. But you are not one of these people. You can erase your fears.

The process of erasing your fears involves becoming aware of your unconscious value system and shifting it around so it works for you rather than against you. This value system is a dual hierarchy of negative and positive feelings existing just below the surface of your awareness. The reason you like doing certain things is that doing them stimulates feelings from your positive values hierarchy. The reason you avoid doing other things is that doing them stimulates feelings from your negative values hierarchy. Internal conflict is caused by activities which stimulate a mixture of positive and negative feelings. If one of the action steps on your plan of action stimulates such a mixture of positive and negative feelings, you will have "mixed emotions" about it, leading to hesitation and procrastination. When you uncover and erase this internal conflict you'll be free to create your dream as easily as you walk to the corner store to buy a loaf of bread. Like a sailor adjusting his sails to take advantage of the wind, the internal changes you make will allow you to take advantage of existing conditions. Your desires will materialize smoothly and easily as a natural byproduct of

173

following your plan as you sail toward your chosen destination.

Here is a strategy for doing this:

How to Erase Your Fears

1 Discover your unconscious value system.

Your positive values are the emotions you like to feel. Asking yourself this question uncovers them:

What's important to me about _____?

Fill in the blank with whatever activity you choose and make a note of the emotion you get as a response.

If the answer you get is something other than an emotion, ask the question about it and keep going until you get to an emotion. For example, if you ask *What's important about working?* and the answer is *Money,* ask yourself, *What's important about money?* If you get the answer, *Buying things,* ask yourself, *What's important about buying things?* If you get the answer, *It makes me feel powerful,* feeling **powerful** is one of your positive values. Ask this question repeatedly about a variety of things until you have created a long list of the positive emotions you like to feel.

Negative values are emotions you try to avoid feeling. To uncover these ask yourself:

What don't I like about _____?

Fill in the blank with any activity you would rather avoid, especially those things you procrastinate in doing that will help achieve your goals. As in the previous example, if the answer is not an emotion, keep going until you get an emotion and make a list of them.

2 Rank your values in order of importance.

Prioritize both lists to become conscious of the most powerful ones. These are your strongest motivating factors and your greatest fears. Associate the positive ones to any activity and you will enjoy it. Associate the negative ones to an activity and you will try to

174

avoid it. Internal conflict comes from needing to do something to which you have associated a negative value.

3 Remove the meaning creating the emotion

Your feelings about things are caused not by the activity itself but by the meaning, which can be changed. Once you have uncovered the activities you avoid and the negative feelings associated with them, ask yourself, What meaning have I given this activity that triggers this feeling in me? Once you have uncovered it, ask yourself, What other meaning could it have?

Use the Affirmation Principle to associate a meaning that erases the negative emotion. This allows you to act freely, opening the door to what you want.

4 Associate a positive emotion to the activity.

Go one step further and give the activity a meaning which stimulates a feeling high on your list of positive values and you will come to enjoy the exact things you used to fear. Over time, this will change your personality and lead to the automatic, unconscious creation of your most desired goals.

Staying on the path

Cultivating the ability to increase your desire, modify your beliefs and erase your fears allows you to maintain a consistent level of self-motivation, taking daily steps in the direction of your goals. Self-motivated people not only take action, they continue acting long after others have quit. You must provide your own reasons for staying on the path in the face of disappointments and difficulties. Fear, lack of clarity or confusion can appear at any point, so at *each step of your journey* you must know not only what you ultimately want and why but also how the next step fits into your overall plan and why you need to take it.

The decisions you make during the Goals Process move from the general to the specific. Initially your desire and belief need be only generally positive and your cost/benefit lists play only a general role in inspiring you to take action. But once you begin your journey it is vital that your feelings be consistent with your goals and plans for each of the countless decisions necessary to follow through on each step of your plan. The key is to keep moving. If the process stops it really makes no difference where or why ... your dream won't happen and you are left watching someone else enjoy the dream that could have been yours. You must continually monitor your present position, your plans, your feelings and your actions. Be prepared to clarify your goals, reaffirm your desire and modify your belief as often as necessary. You will have to overcome a series of fears on your journey but ultimately all your work will pay off. In the meantime you must do what's necessary to motivate yourself to take the next step.

When you have cultivated a high level of awareness and clarity concerning your goals, your plans and your highest motivating values and when you have eliminated your fear of taking action you will have removed all roadblocks to your success. You will have empowered yourself to create the opportunities which are the structuring causes for the manifestation of your dreams. You will have developed a level of personal power that makes others sit up and take notice. You will be free to create your dream and free to enjoy your success.

Chapter Twenty Two

Using Your Imagination

Imagination is more important than knowledge.

Albert Einstein

Your Plan of Action may eventually become the most detailed thing you've ever created in your life, and it should be! After all, isn't it the blueprint for the life of your dreams? If you were building your dream house, wouldn't you want the builder to have a detailed blueprint of every square foot of the finished structure? If you were financing a movie, wouldn't you expect the shooting script to contain every detail of the finished film? Of course you would! Is designing your life any less important? If you are truly committed to using your power to create your life, your plan had better be detailed.

The ability to think clearly and plan effectively is fundamental to the success of every writer, architect, inventor, artist, scientist and business person. Consistent work in your binder will develop this skill to a high degree. Your lists of possible and actual goals and the obstacles you need to deal with will provide you with plenty of raw material to create a very detailed plan. As your plan develops, the increasingly detailed action steps will tell you where applying the magic of your mind will have the most effect.

Using your imagination as a creative force

Are you using your imagination or is it using you? Is it an aid to clarifying your goals and designing your plans or are you being victimized by its uncontrolled wanderings through the infinitely broad spectrum of possible futures laid out before you? The information entering your mind from the future will determine how you feel, influence how motivated you are to either follow or

177

abandon your plan and control your conception of how possible your dreams are and how difficult or how easy it will be to create them.

Fear, worry, confusion, muddled thinking, a low level of motivation, sagging confidence, low self-esteem and negative emotions are all unmistakable indicators that your imagination is out of control, that the ideas and feelings you experience are a product of your undisciplined thinking. Lets face it: you wouldn't feel badly if you had a choice. So negative feelings and confused, fuzzy thinking indicate that you need to practice controlling the focus of your inner awareness.

The ability to control the focus of your inner awareness and to visualize various aspects of your goals in advance will be a tremendous aid to planning your life and a vital aid in uncovering the feelings you have unconsciously associated to each of the steps in your plan. As you clarify your goals, you will know precisely where to place the focus of your awareness, drawing from this area of the inner future the information you need to act effectively. Incorporating an ongoing series of daily visualization exercises into your daily plan of action will help guarantee that you use the creative power of your mind in the most effective and efficient manner. Here's how to incorporate your imagination as an integral part of the daily process of creating your dreams.

Experience your chosen future in advance

Each of the action steps necessary to accomplish your long-range goals already exists in the inner future as a possible event, a virtual reality on your possible world line, marking the road to your ultimate destination. By connecting with these virtual realities through your imagination you can experience each of them in advance, helping you make the decisions and adjustments necessary to guarantee that you experience them in the physical world.

To create your dream you will need to make a conscious decision to let each of these intermediate steps manifest as a

178

physical reality in your life, taking responsibility for making the subtle internal adjustments to your beliefs and feelings as necessary to accept the manifestation of each step. To not do this on an ongoing basis would be like driving your car without paying attention to the road. You might end up hitting a pothole, or worse yet, driving into the ditch! You don't want that to happen. Without paying attention to the subtle feelings associated to each intermediate step, an unconscious fear may cause you to procrastinate, keeping them from materializing.

This conscious use of your imagination to help create your dream is a skill you must cultivate or your imagination will seize control and feed you information and ideas you don't want. This technique has several aspects to it and you need to master them all.

Constantly practice the art of projecting your inner awareness to the point in inner space-time where the next step in your plan *has already been reached*. By pretending it has already materialized, you will experience the feelings you are unconsciously associating to the imagined event. If the feelings are positive, you can relax, and enjoy the experience, knowing your unconscious mind is allowing your plan to move along toward your goal. But any *negative feelings* you notice indicate an unconscious fear is operating, trying to keep the event you desire from materializing. If you deny this subtle internal conflict and don't deal with these negative feelings, you will be unconsciously preventing your dream from materializing.

Part of this process involves using the  Affirmation Principle to uncover and remove the references supporting this fear and these negative feelings. Another part of the process involves allowing yourself to experience the positive benefits you expect as *positive feelings* in your body before your goal is actually accomplished. This taste of success increases your desire and helps motivate you to stay on the path.

If you project your inner awareness to a point in a parallel future where you've failed to achieve your goal you can *experience the feeling of having failed.* Imagine watching someone else enjoy the dream you could have created for yourself and feel the failure feelings. Intensify them five times ... ten times ... This will help motivate you to stay on the path, since your desire to avoid these negative feelings will be a strong motivating force in keeping you from abandoning your plan. Be sure to work all sides of this exercise as an ongoing aspect of your daily success routine.

The whole process looks like the following:

Using your imagination as a creative force

- Choose the outcome you desire.
- List the benefits of succeeding and the costs of failing.
- Uncover your positive and negative values hierarchy.
- Eliminate any negative feelings associated to this outcome.
- Imagine yourself at the point in inner space-time where you have <u>achieved your goal</u> enjoying the positive feelings of having succeeded.
- Imagine yourself at a point in inner space-time where you have <u>failed</u>, experiencing your negative values hierarchy.
- Repeat this exercise until you automatically associate your highest positive values to succeeding and your highest negative values to failing.

Include this visualization process as part of your daily program. Spend a few minutes each day using your imagination to work all sides of the process. Keep a diary of your efforts with this technique or you will forget to practice it.

I can't overemphasize the importance of cultivating this skill.

Epilogue

I began this book with a discussion of an inner process which creates our life below the level of our normal conscious awareness. I then outlined a series of techniques we can use to become conscious of this process and some exercises to aid us in directing it.

We now have a new conceptual framework with which to understand our world and our mind and the connection between the two. We have a new way of understanding ourselves and of the part we each play in the creation of our personal reality.

We have tools to analyze our attitudes. We have a way to cultivate empowering beliefs. We know how our emotions and states influence our perceptions and we have a technique to eliminate negative emotions and cultivate positive ones. We know how to design our Fantasy Lifestyle, how to break it down to a series of specific, balanced goals and how to design a detailed Plan of Action to achieve them.

We know how to project the inner awareness to any point in the past and to direct the focus of the awareness by asking questions, giving us new tools to learn new lessons from the past, thereby transforming an experience we once thought was negative into one that empowers us.

We know how to project the inner awareness to any point in the future, including one when our dream actually exists, thereby gaining access to the information necessary to bring our dream into reality. We know how to create a filing system to keep track of all the great ideas that come flooding into our mind in ever increasing numbers. We know how to remain motivated as we use these new ides to create the life of our choice.

We know how to systematically cultivate a new personality, how to eliminate negative personality traits and how to cultivate positive ones. Making a conscious decision to participate in this process of conscious co-creation involves us in a spiral of increasing awareness, increasing responsibility and increasing power. This process begins by transforming and healing our inner life, but soon spreads out to touch the lives of our loved ones and the people with whom we come into contact.

As my awareness and ability have grown, I have come to realize that healing myself involves not only forgiving those who have unconsciously harmed me. It also gives me an opportunity to help in healing those who have come before me and those who will come after me. I have realized that I am merely one link in a great chain of being that stretches from before time into the endless future.

The adventure is just beginning. Enjoy it.

Anthony's You Tube site contains a series of videos which explain various parts of the theory of consciousness explained in this book. Check them out at:

http://www.youtube.com/user/TonyinChina

About the Author

Anthony Hamilton is a certified law of attraction trainer, seminar leader, personal vision coach and philosopher. At the age of 10 he had a vision, in which he saw himself at the age of 35. This vision became progressively real, both the good he was looking forward to and the bad he was trying to avoid. Since having knowledge of the future is supposed to be impossible, he was inspired to spend fifteen years exploring the nature of consciousness to discover how such a memory of the future could happen.

In the process he discovered that knowledge of the future is always available to us but that for most of us our beliefs create a blind spot which hides the information from us.

He spent a number of years discovering a way to systematically peel back the layers of thinking and belief that were preventing information from our "future memory" from reaching conscious awareness.

Mind, Time and Power! details his discovery.

Anthony is a graduate of the University of British Columbia (Philosophy). His daughter Alecia is a nurse. His son Graham is a film-maker in Vancouver.

For information on Anthony's recorded programs and live training seminars, contact him at:

http://www.anthonyhamilton.org

The above site also contains links and resources to help you create the life of your choice.

183

Notes

Notes

Notes